1978

PEOPLES OF THE EARTH

volume **1** Australia and Melanesia (including New Guinea)

volume **2** Africa from the Sahara to the Zambesi

volume **3** Europe (including USSR west of the Urals)

volume **4** Mexico and Central America

volume **5** Islands of the Atlantic (including the Caribbean)

volume **6** Amazonia, Orinoco and pampas

volume **7** Andes

volume **8** The Pacific – Polynesia and Micronesia

volume **9** Southern Africa and Madagascar

volume **10** Indonesia, Philippines and Malaysia

volume **11** South-East Asia

volume **12** The Indian subcontinent (including Ceylon)

volume **13** China (including Tibet), Japan and Korea

volume **14** USSR east of the Urals

volume **15** Western and central Asia

volume **16** The Arctic

volume **17** The Arab World

volume **18** North America

volume **19** Man the craftsman

volume **20** The Future of Mankind. General Index

volume fourteen **USSR** East of the Urals

THE DANBURY PRESS

Contents

Supervisory Editor of the Series:
Professor Sir Edward Evans-Pritchard,
Fellow of All Souls, Professor of Social Anthropology,
University of Oxford, 1946-1970,
Chevalier de la Légion d'Honneur

Volume Editor:
Dr Caroline Humphrey,
Girton College, University of Cambridge

Preceding Page
Bleak, frozen Siberia was
once known as the 'Land of
White Silence'. Now the 20th
century and discoveries of
valuable mineral deposits have
transformed vast once-
forbidding territories into a
potential treasure-house and
Russia's new land of
opportunity.

The DANBURY PRESS
a division of GROLIER ENTERPRISES INC.

Publisher
ROBERT B. CLARKE

Printed in Italy by
Arnoldo Mondadori Editore, Verona

8–11 Animals and man: the biological roots of society

Hilary Callan, MA, B Litt, Dip Soc Anth, author of *Ethnology and Society: Towards an Anthropological View*

12–13 Peoples of Siberia and Mongolia

Dr Caroline Humphrey, Girton College, University of Cambridge

14–43 Peoples of Mongolia

Dr Caroline Humphrey

44–47 Shamanism

David Felton

48–51 Khanti and Mansi – Khanti-Mansi National Okrug

P J Lineton, BA, Scott Polar Research Institute, Cambridge

52–55 Nentsi – Northern Siberia

John Massey Stewart, MA(Cantab), FRGS, Hon. Lib. The Royal Central Asian Society, author of *Across the Russias* etc

56–69 Yakut – Yakut ASSR

Dr T E Armstrong, Scott Polar Research Institute, Cambridge, author of *Russian Settlement in the North* etc

70–73 Altai – Gorno-Altai Autonomous Oblast

Ethel Dunn, Executive Secretary, Highgate Road Social Science Research Station, Berkeley, California, co-author of *Peasants of Central Russia*

74–77 Tsaatang – Mongolia

Dr Caroline Humphrey

Siberian Russians

78–86 The Pioneers

Douglas Botting, MA(Oxon), FRGS, producer of BBC documentary about Siberia, author of *One Chilly Siberian Morning*

87–103 The new Siberians

Stephen le Fleming and Rosalind le Fleming

104–105 Udege – Khabarovaskii Kray and Maritime Kray

Dr Violet Conolly, OBE, Member of the Council of the Royal Central Asian Society, author of *Beyond the Urals*

106–109 Tuvintsi – Tuva Autonomous Oblast

P J Lineton, BA

110–117 Evenki – Siberia

Dr Violet Conolly, OBE

118–123 Buriat – Buriat-Mongol Okrug

Dr Caroline Humphrey

124–125 Ket – Yenitsei river, southern Siberia

P J Lineton, BA

126–129 Nivkhi – Bureinskiy Khrebet and Sakhalin

Ethel Dunn

130–135 Koryak – Kamchatka

Ethel Dunn

136–144 Glossary to the peoples of Siberia and Mongolia

STAFF CREDITS
Editorial Director **Tom Stacey**
Picture Director **Alexander Low**
Executive Editor **Katherine Ivens**
Art Director **Tom Deas**
Assistant Editor **Elisabeth Meakin**
Project Co-ordinator **Anne Harrison**
Research **Cheryl Moyer**

Specialist Picture Research **Claire Baines**
Picture Research **Elly Beintema/Diana Eggitt**
Jeanne Griffiths/Carolyn Keay/Emma Stacey
Editorial Assistants **Richard Carlisle/Rosamund Ellis**
J M Marrin/Susan Rutherford/Pamela Tubby
Editorial Secretary **Caroline Silverman**
Design Assistants **Susan Forster/Richard Kelly**
Cartography **Ron Hayward**
Illustrations **Sandra Archibald, Ron McTrusty**

Production **Roger Multon**
Production Editor **Vanessa Charles**

The publishers gratefully acknowledge help from
the following organizations:
Royal Anthropological Institute, London
Musée de l'Homme, Paris
International African Institute, London
British Museum, London
Royal Geographical Society, London
Scott Polar Research Institute, Cambridge
Royal Asiatic Society, London
Royal Central Asian Society, London
Pitt-Rivers Museum, Oxford
Horniman Museum, London
Institute of Latin American Studies, London

PICTURE CREDITS
Cover: **Philip Jones Griffiths, Bonatti and de Biasi** (Mondadori), **Elliott Erwitt** (Magnum from the John Hillelson Agency). **Arctic Institute of North America** 72. **Bayliss and Botting** (Camera Press) 66 cr. **Jorgen Bitsch** (Black Star, New York) 74 – 75, 80 tl, 85 b, 87 tl, 88, 89 tl, 94 bl, 95 b, 96. **Jorgen Bitsch** (ZEFA) 34, 35, 38 t, 40 t, 41, 76, 77. **Bonatti and de Biasi** (Mondadori) 56 – 57, 58, 60, 61 b, 62 – 63, 64 bl, 65. **Camera Press** 67, 132 tl. **Jerry Cooke** 80 cl, 84 r, 87 tr, 92 tr, 94 br, 95 t. **Kai Donners** (National Museum of Finland) 48 b, 51 l, 55 c. **Harrison Forman** (F.P.G.) 40 bl, 42. **F.P.G.** 44. **Martine Franck** (Viva) 68 t, 100 cl, 103 b. **Hamburg Museum of Mankind** 47 b, 48 t, 49, 50, 51 r, 55 t, 108, 124 through 127, 128 br, 129 tl. From the John Hillelson Agency – **Howard Sochurek** 17, 18 – 19, 22 l, 24 tl, 27 cr, 29, 30 tl, 38 br, 39, 43, 68 tl & r, 69. Gamma from the John Hillelson Agency – **Bernard Hermann** 20 t & bl, 24 c & bl, 24 r, 25, 27 t & cl and tr, 28, 30 bl, 31 br, 32, 33. Magnum from the John Hillelson Agency – **Elliott Erwitt** 84 l, 87 b, 92 tl & br, 93, 97 tl, **Burt Glinn** 2 – 3, 78 – 79, 82, 83 l, 89 r, 91, 97 r, 100 br, 101, 102, **Marc Riboud** 16 b, 36 r, 37. **Philip Jones Griffiths** 14 – 15, 22 t & br. **Hans Kramarz** (ZEFA) 40 br. **John Launois** (Black Star, New York) 83 br, 90. **Stephen le Fleming** 98 – 99. **E J Lindgren** 111 through 115, 117. **Mansell Collection** 27 br. **Fred J Maroon** (Louis Mercier) 16 t, 20 r, 21, 36 l. **John Massey Stewart** 31 t, 89 bl. **Musée de l'Homme** 45, 47 t, 54, 118 through 121, 123 tr, 128 t. **Novosti Press Agency** 52 – 53, 105 tr. **L Garkavi** 134 t. Novosti from F.P.G. – **O Ivanov** 122 tl, **M Kukhtarev** 107, **V Minkevich** 105 bl, **V Polunin** 55 b, **S Solovyev** 66 cl, **V Yakoulev** 66 t. **Pitt-Rivers Museum** 130 – 131, 132 b. **Paul Popper** 47 c, 116, 129 cl, 134 b. **Radio Times Hulton Picture Library** 73, 122 bl, 123 br. **George St George** (Laurence Pollinger Ltd) 135. **Emil Schulthess** (Black Star, New York) 59, 61 t, 80 r, 100 bl. **Snark International** 64 tl. **Society for Cultural Relations with USSR.** 105 tl. **Yuri Somov** (Camera Press) 103 tl. **Roger Viollet** 70 – 71. **Peter Wickman** 83 t & cr.
Key: **t**=top, **c**=centre, **b**=bottom, **r**=right, **l**=left.

Peoples of the Earth, volumes one to twenty

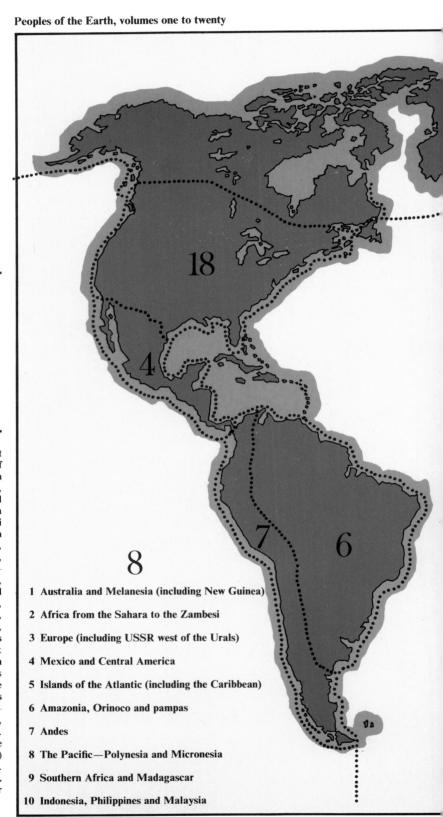

1 Australia and Melanesia (including New Guinea)

2 Africa from the Sahara to the Zambesi

3 Europe (including USSR west of the Urals)

4 Mexico and Central America

5 Islands of the Atlantic (including the Caribbean)

6 Amazonia, Orinoco and pampas

7 Andes

8 The Pacific—Polynesia and Micronesia

9 Southern Africa and Madagascar

10 Indonesia, Philippines and Malaysia

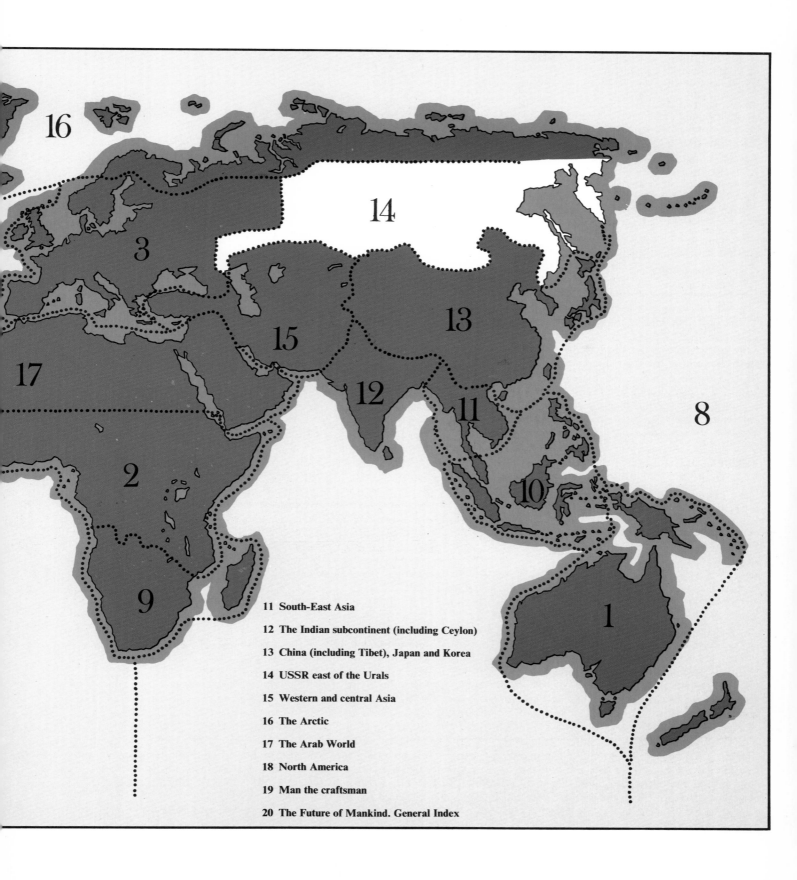

11 South-East Asia

12 The Indian subcontinent (including Ceylon)

13 China (including Tibet), Japan and Korea

14 USSR east of the Urals

15 Western and central Asia

16 The Arctic

17 The Arab World

18 North America

19 Man the craftsman

20 The Future of Mankind. General Index

Animals and man: the biological roots of society

We cannot consider the relationship of mankind with other animals entirely objectively. We have inherited a tradition of assumptions which gives man a unique position in the material and moral universe. Although we may no longer consciously share our for-fathers' man-centered view of the world many of its implications must still, often at an unconscious level, affect our thinking. This may be partly because we have not yet replaced the man-centered view with an entirely coherent world view of our own.

Man has of course always known that he is in some sense an animal. Aristotle remarked 'Man is a political animal' (though this is said to be a poor translation) around 340 BC. Western intellectual man has, for centuries been uneasily aware of a kinship between himself and the rest of the animal world. His awareness of this kinship with animals makes him uneasy for several reasons, of which the simplest is the straightforward threat which recognition of his animal nature might present to his sense of uniqueness – his dignity almost – as a man. He could not but see himself as akin to the higher animals, especially to monkeys, in bodily form and function, and in certain basic patterns of behavior such as eating, sleeping and mating. But at the same time, on the philosophical and theoretical plane, he could not but consider himself uniquely rational. He could not but see himself as the possessor of a soul, or as even the product of a divine act of creation. Traditional philosophy sharply separated mind from matter. Man's soul and his higher intellectual faculties belonged on one side of this impenetrable barrier; his body and its functions, and the rest of the material world, on the other.

This dualistic tradition is yet another impediment to examining the link between man and animals objectively. Whenever an intellectual system creates sharp distinctions between one category of things and another, it appears that a peculiar significance tends to be attached to anything which fails to fit neatly into either category. Anything which possesses characteristics of both categories seems to undermine the foundations of the intellectual system itself. It tends to acquire a special ritual status or to become a focus for peculiar attitudes – a deep abhorrence or a compulsive fascination. It is a tendency which anthropologists have observed over a wide range of topics and of societies. Given our anthropocentric (man-centered) habits of thought it is not surprising that we should contemplate with some degree of anxious fascination any observations which tend to blur the distinction between man and animal.

Objective observation of the areas in which our behavior resembles that of other animals has to overcome such intellectual obstacles. What intellectual gains can we expect from such an enterprise? The one I want to consider concerns the value, for the study of society, of applying to human social behavior and organization what we can call biological thinking. Biological thinking involves the evolutionary question of how human society in general came to be the way it is, and comparison of the human with other species.

Taking the human species as a whole to be a product of the evolutionary process, elements of human society which appear to be common to all cultures are selected; then, drawing on evidence of human pre-history, attempts are made to trace the types of selection pressure which acted on our primate and pre-human ancestors to produce these constant elements. It appears, for example, that our remote ancestors evolved, both in body and in behavior, in relation to a forest-dwelling vegetarian way of life. At some point in evolutionary time they moved to an open savanna habitat, with an economy partly based on meat-eating. This meant that the evolving pre-hominid, in order to compete with the large well-equipped carnivores which were already exploiting this new ecological niche, had to draw on the primate capacities he already possessed and put them to new uses. The primate's interest in manipulating objects and his rudimentary capacity for using tools (which one can observe in modern chimpanzees) was developed into a more sophisticated tool and weapon technology. The primate talent for social communication and organization was channeled and disciplined. Co-operative hunting groups formed and habits of sharing food and dividing labor developed which were all essential to the new way of life – although this is of course a gross over-simplification.

This type of investigation, which rests on paleontological and other evidence of human evolution, has potentially great significance in interpreting apparently constant features of human society, such as men's constant tendency to bond together in groups that exclude women. Close study of living non-human primates is necessary to gain some idea of the common core of primate tendencies on which specifically human ways of doing things were grafted.

Looking at mankind comparatively, as one species among many, reveals certain broad uniformities which derive from man's evolution. For the zoologist including *homo sapiens* among the species he studies is simply a matter of completeness. He finds it unsatisfying and untidy to single out one species for special neglect, just because he happens to belong to it himself. For the anthropologist, whose job it is to analyze human society and culture, the implications of a comparative biological approach may be far more wide-reaching. So great is the diversity of human institutions the world over that the anthropologist who is immersed in the details of particular communities and their variations is easily led to think of human society itself as totally arbitrary. So indeed it may be.

A comparative biological perspective will however open our eyes to the constants of human society. And it will counteract our traditional preoccupation with the varieties of human society. There is a widespread tendency, for example, for exclusive all-male groups to form within a society. Whether these take the form of secret men's clubs, as in many simple societies, or in freemasonry, as in Europe and America, or just gatherings of men in which women are made to feel unwelcome, there seems to be a pressure towards their existence in some form. It is this pressure, not the groups themselves, which needs to be considered. A biological interpretation would begin by surveying the general tendency among primates, especially monkeys, for males to bond together into sub-groups whose members, while they may compete for status, also co-operate in important ways. This bonding tendency seems to have considerable survival value for the group. It maintains order within it and defends it. As primates became hunters this tendency of males to bond together probably became the basis of the co-operative hunting group. The importance of this male bond made it necessary to protect it from any interference from the male-female bond. Hence, perhaps, the exclusion of females from male groups. What is significant is not that the nature of these groups is determined in any rigid sense, but that the behavior tendencies which we share with many primates predisposes us to form male groups and makes it easy for groups of this type to form within societies.

Other examples of the basic, perhaps biologically-based, uniformities which underlie all cultures can be found in the familiar rituals of everyday life. Greeting ceremonies, for example, vary enormously from the most formal to the most intimate. But their very prevalence suggests some sort of biological predisposition. And something like greeting occurs in most non-human primates, and in many other animals as well. Everyone is familiar with the greeting behavior of the dog. It seems likely that in social animals greeting may have evolved as a way of maintaining and consolidating the social structure, and also of expressing relevant facts about the relationship between individuals – such as their relative status – when they meet.

It must be emphasized that biological hypotheses based on comparative evidence neither rule out nor in any sense replace other kinds of explanation. A number of those who have written about the links between human and animal behavior have overstressed animal comparisons in their explanations of human affairs. Although *homo sapiens* may or may not be among the species which respond to the territorial imperative, for example, nationalism is not reducible to territorial instincts.

Let us examine more closely the nature of biological thinking, and some of its findings. Ethology is the name now given to that branch of zoology which concerns itself with behavior, and has largely replaced the older term 'comparative psychology'. Ethology is the better of the two terms, so far as terms are important, because it suggests no relation of this science to psychology. Psychologists and ethologists are both interested in behavior, but their ways of studying it are different. The experimental psychologist selects a topic such as learning or perception and explores it experimentally, under strict laboratory conditions, through the medium of an animal. The ethologist by contrast does not try nearly so hard to control all variables. Being a zoologist he begins with the animal. He is interested in it as a total functioning organism, and sees body and behavior as an interlocking whole, shaped by the evolutionary process to meet the needs of a given environment.

This is not to suggest that the ethologist does not do experiments: he can and frequently does. But the experiment usually follows prolonged and intensive observation of the animal in conditions as close as possible to the natural habitat. Only then do the relevant problems shape themselves in his mind. From his long immersion in animal-watching he may emerge with a fact which requires explanation and a hypothesis to explain it; and a judicious experiment will often clinch the matter. When the Dutch ethologist Niko Tinbergen was studying the black-headed gull he was struck by the care with which the parent birds removed all traces of egg-shell from the area of the nest after the chicks had hatched. He speculated that this behavior, by removing tell-tale signs that would otherwise attract predators to the nest, might have survival value, and he was in fact able to prove this experimentally.

Ethology has existed as a science only within this century. It takes its theoretical framework from the post-Darwinian biology of which it is a branch. Ethologists tend automatically to look for explanations for what they observe along traditional Darwinian lines of function, causation and survival. This has meant that ethologists have in the past concentrated their attention on animal species such as insects, fish and birds whose behavior is relatively fixed or genetically determined. When they have turned to animals whose behavior is more complex and dependent on individual learning they have often singled out patterns of behavior signalling systems whereby animals communicate their mood and intentions to one another, which can be shown to have a large element of genetic determination.

When ethologists have tried to apply their techniques to human social behavior this habit of concentrating first on individual behavior and second on those acts which are 'inbuilt' has led to rather disappointing results. Too often the enquiry has degenerated into a rather pointless brawl about whether or not there are any 'instincts' in man. Now it would be very surprising if man did not possess some behavioral signs of his primate ancestry. It is almost beyond doubt that certain elements of human 9 non-verbal communication – postures, gestures, facial expression – are inbuilt in the sense that they are reliable indications of the individual's motives, regardless of cultural variation. And among animals it is common to find that an individual animal can present a stimulus which triggers an automatic, unlearned response in another. There is good reason to believe that human beings possess several such inbuilt responses. The combination of a rounded form, for example, with a head that is large in relation to the body, and with a small face and clumsy movements immediately suggests in human eyes a 'baby' – whether a child, a puppy, or a kitten – and usually calls forth protective parental responses.

There seem, then, to be some continuities between human and animal behavior. Pointing out where these lie has traditionally been about the limit of the ethologists' contribution to the study of man. My own view is that while these comparisons illuminate human behavior, they are, unless the analysis can be pushed further, of limited interest in understanding human society. Recently there has been a virtual revolution in ethology which has produced the capacity and the enthusiasm for analyzing social systems. Faced with the sheer complexity of primate society, the ethologist has been forced to adopt more sophisticated concepts than that of behavior alone.

There are three phenomena related to tradition, kinship and politics, which are all considered 'building blocks' of human society. Each of these has also been found somewhere or other among the non-human primates.

Many animals have a tradition of information about local conditions which is passed on by one generation to the next. Jackdaws teach their young to avoid notorious predators and even to recognize the local poacher. The reason why the life-span in some animals extends well beyond the breeding age, which is apparently a luxury for any species, may be that it is an advantage to have some aged individuals who will know how to cope with a rare dire emergency. If for example a severe drought occurs only once in 15-20 years, there is a good chance that a very old baboon will remember the way to a distant water-hole which was last resorted to in his youth. It is rare, however, to have the opportunity to watch a process of innovation becoming a tradition.

But this did occur among the Japanese monkeys of Koshima Island. This wild group of monkeys has been studied for many years. In 1952 the primatologist began scattering sweet potatoes on the beach, and a young female invented the technique of washing the potatoes to remove the sand from them before eating them. It became a habit which spread throughout the group, so that it is now a characteristic of that particular troupe. What is interesting is how the habit spread, from the original female to her age-mates, from juveniles to mothers, and later from mothers to their young. The

adult males of that generation never learned the techniques. Here, then, the development of the tradition was a function of the total social system of the group of monkeys and of each individual monkey's place within it. The study of the Japanese monkeys also illustrated kinship and its influence on social behavior. Animal, like human societies, do not exist in a timeless limbo. The Japanese monkeys are among the few groups to have been studied over a long period. Really long-term observation over several generations is essential to understand the development of the complex network of relationships and alliances which exist at any one moment.

The Japanese researchers found that the influence of kinship in determining social status among the Japanese monkeys is very strong. Monkeys do not have a relation of paternity. The male-female bond is usually temporary and depends on the female's phase in the reproductive cycle. So monkey kinship ties are usually through the mother. The researchers found that if you knew the position of a female in the hierarchy of dominance – or the pecking order – you could predict fairly accurately the status which would ultimately be attained by her young. Not only does the young monkey apparently learn the habits of dominant or submissive behavior from his mother. A dominant mother will spend much of her time close to the powerful males who run things and as her infant matures they will 'get to know its face'. They will be more tolerant towards it than towards the child of a low status mother. For the ambitious monkey, as for man, rule number one can be to 'choose the right family'. Similar regularities have been described in other primate species.

Something even more interesting happens among some Javanese (crab-eating) monkeys which were observed in a zoo colony. Not only is status in the colony largely dependent on kinship, but the support a monkey can muster in a fight or confrontation is a close reflection of these kinship ties. This surely is the beginning of political organization. Kinship ties in a monkey group gain a political function in the resolution of conflicts. Whether or not this is a general feature of primate life we do not yet know. Hierarchies of dominance – 'pecking orders' is an older expression – have long been known to exist in many very different kinds of animal. The chicken is the classic example. The individual chicken in any barnyard knows exactly who can peck her with impunity and whom she may peck in turn. This means that different chickens have different access to food, to space and often to survival.

It was once thought that order or rank arose entirely from aggressive behavior. Experiments would be staged in which two animals would be placed in competitive confrontation to see which won. But recent studies of primate societies, however, have revealed that the situation is infinitely more complex. Although aggressive status-seeking certainly goes on, especially among the baboons and other monkeys there are, in some species, forces which bind the groups into a cohesive whole through the attraction which dominant animals hold for the other members. Each animal maintains a constant awareness of the behavior of the 'key individuals' throughout his waking day and co-ordinates his movements with theirs. 'Leadership' comes about not as a result of bullying but as a logical consequence of this 'attention structure' as it has been called. Status can be gained by attention-getting displays, and by skilful manipulation of relationships. This is a genuinely political process. And it is a much more interesting explanation than the old theory of dominance and individual aggressive potential.

To plan any social maneuver a monkey has to weigh up a number of factors. Where are the dominant monkeys and where are his friends? What mood are they in? Are they likely to be annoyed by his maneuver? Or might it even be possible to exploit a dominant monkey by coming up close to him and from this position threatening a rival who dare not threaten back? If the indications are that he should be discreet our monkey may have to suppress his impulse, however strong. Add to this the alliance based on individual friendship and on kinship, and you can see that in order to 'make out' in this type of society a monkey has to be a very smooth political operator indeed.

It would therefore be quite wrong for the general reader to get the impression that because the typical primate society is hierarchical, the 'blueprint' for primate social life is of aggressive, competitive, exploitative status-seeking. This would be a totally inadequate description of monkey society and a totally inadequate 'biological model' of human social life. Monkey societies are typically *political*. Thereby hangs a paradox of considerable interest for the study of man.

It is a paradox which we can best approach by considering what non-human primates do not do in the wild. We are so used to thinking of monkeys and apes as near-human that it comes as a surprise to realize that certain types of adaptive, apparently very simple, behavior are not found among them under natural conditions. Primates apart from man do not, even with their own young, share food. They do not store food. They do not build shelters, apart from the makeshift one-night sleeping platforms constructed by the anthropoid apes. Most birds can do better. They have no real technology. Although wild chimpanzees will prepare and use sticks for probing termite nests this is not impressive compared to what the same animals will achieve in captivity. And this is the point: monkeys and apes in captivity can be taught skills, and reveal capacities, for which there is no obvious function in nature. They can do far more than they do do.

Possibly the most interesting explanation why this is so is the suggestion that it was the complex nature of primate society itself which stimulated the evolution of the primate's inventive brain. Primate intelligence is not designed for technical application at all. But it can be put to use as a secondary adaptation in performing complex technical tasks. This is shown by the feats performed by captive monkeys and apes. By an extension of the hypothesis, this is what happened in human evolution: we owe our own mastery of the physical environment to our pre-human ancestors' social accomplishments.

The reader will immediately recognize how startling this idea is. Assuming that man evolved from a primate whose habits resembled those of living monkeys and apes, the big brain, responsible for every human achievement, developed first of all in response to pressures which came from within society – and specifically from the political nature of that society.

Let us try to draw together some of the threads of this essay. For many years ethology has offered alternatives to the environmentalist, 'tabula rasa' attitude to human behavior – which regarded the infant mind as a 'blank slate' on which anything consistent with the laws of learning could be written. Ethologists have consistently argued that on biological grounds it would be most surprising if this were so. They have presented a good case for saying that certain elements of human social behavior are comparable with those of other animals, that they are genetically influenced and that they have come to exist as a result of evolutionary mechanisms. Latterly they have begun to do something more exciting. They have analyzed social systems in animals. Perhaps the most general lesson for the anthropologist here is that society is, far from being sharply distinct from nature, a part of nature in important ways. Biology and society flow into one another. The old distinction between nature and culture is, to put it mildly, blurred.

A final philosophical problem raises its head. If we can show on ethological grounds that pressures exist towards the formation of one kind of institution rather than another – as perhaps with all-male groups – does this force us to take a deterministic view of society: to hold that such institutions are inevitable and unchangeable? A number of popularizers of ethology have written as if the social biology of man compelled a conservative, even a reactionary, political stance. My own view would be more moderate, and would lay stress on the versatility of primates and their capacity to adapt to new demands. But it is up to the interested reader to survey the evidence and decide for himself. The field is wide open.

Peoples of Siberia and Mongolia

Siberia is often imagined an area of desolate forest and tundra, unimaginably cold, barren and inhospitable, peopled only by infrequent, wandering tribes. There is, some think, no more dismal place on earth.

One cannot sum up Siberia like this. It varies geographically from arid southern steppe, hot in summer, to Arctic tundra with permanently frozen subsoil. There are rice fields in the river valleys of the far east, reindeer herds in the Altai and Sayan mountains in the south, and cattle and horse ranches in the central north of Yakutia. While small co-operatives of hunters and fur-trappers still roam the forests, there are also great historic cities, industrial areas, university and academic towns and huge hydro-electric schemes. The majority of Siberians are Russians, many of whom have roots in the area going back several centuries. The 'tribes' include descendants of the great Asian empires of the past, the Mongols, Turks and Tatars. The Mordva, Khanti and Mansi for example, are relatives of European peoples such as the Finns and Hungarians. The variety of geographical regions, cultures and languages is enormous. According to some estimates there are at least 64 native peoples of Siberia, not counting Russians, Ukrainians, Germans and others who have settled there.

This volume aims to give a picture of the present and past ways of life of a representative selection of these peoples and also those of the Mongolian People's Republic, which is an independent country, an ally of the Soviet Union with its own representative at the UN.

The Soviets divide Siberia into three regions: west Siberia, from the Urals to the Yenisey; east Siberia, from the Yenisey to Trans-Baikalia, and the far east from Trans-Baikalia to the Pacific. These regions used to be administered separately by the Tsarist government. Now they are all included in the immense Russian Soviet Federated Socialist Republic. Decisions are made in Moscow, 4,000 or 5,000 miles away and delays and roundaboutness in bureaucratic matters are inevitable. On the other hand centralization has enabled the Soviet government to try to establish a common standard of living over this vast territory. In important matters like legal status, politics, medical services and education, conditions have as far as possible been standardized. Centralization has also enabled the government to take special measures to deal with the problems created by Siberia's relative underpopulation, transport difficulties, varied cultures, economies and so on. For example, while wages were kept level in the rest of the USSR they were raised substantially in certain parts of Siberia to encourage immigration. When a regional economy such as reindeer herding began to lose its viability, the central government was able to raise the price of reindeer meat.

Soviet scholars distinguish five main physical types of Siberian native peoples which do not necessarily correspond to their three main language groups: Paleoasiatic, Uralic and Altaic. The Uralics, for example the west Siberian Khanti and Mansi, the Sel'kup and the western Nentsi, have light skin and eyes, soft straight hair, a slight epicanthine fold, body hair, low height (averaging $5\frac{1}{2}$ feet in men) and medium head measurements. The Baikal or Paleo-Siberian, for example the Amur and Sakhalin Evenki and certain of the Yakut, have a strongly developed epicanthine fold, thin lips, a very long upper lip, prominent cheek-bones and varying head measurements. The Central-Asiatic, for example the Buriat, Yakut, northern Mongols, Tuvintsi, Shor, Altain and the Khakass have darkly pigmented skin, stronger hair growth than the Baikal type and a higher skull, lowish stature and a well developed epicanthine fold. The Amur-Sakhalin, for example the Nivkhi, Ul'chi and some of the Orochi have dark pigmentation of hair, eyes and skin, a developed epicanthine fold, body hair, high wide faces with prominent cheek-bones, wide lips, medium and round head measurements and low stature. The Arctic or Eskimo group, such as the Chukchi, Koryak and Itel'men have slight development of the epicanthus, relatively thick body hair, swarthy skin and thick lips.

Linguistic and physical anthropological data show that the native peoples have been interacting, moving and changing throughout their history. Many, the Khanti and Mansi for example, have apparently come from much further south, as far even as the Aral sea region, where they must have led a different way of life. Others, such as the Yakut, have mixed physical characteristics including Central-Asiatic, Baikal and European traits. Their language too is mixed. It has a Turkic base with Mongol and Paleoasiatic elements. The numbers of peoples involved in this area are so small that it is not surprising that their numbers and ways of life were so unstable.

Are the native Siberians dying out? At the beginning of the century Russian demographers concluded that the peoples who lived in barren regions and areas – where agriculture was difficult – were decreasing. However the natives living in river valleys and southern agricultural regions were increasing, despite famines and epidemics.

Many Siberian peoples are now increasing rapidly. The Tuvintsi of Tuva, ASSR, grew from 98,000 in 1959 to 135,000 in 1970, and the Buriat of Buriat ASSR grew from 136,000 in 1959 to 178,000 in 1970. But other groups especially the smallest, barely hold their own. It is probable that the Aleut, for example, now about 400 strong, are too small to survive as an ethnic unit.

The great majority of the native Siberians are still living in their home territories. Their activities are not unlike those of their ancestors. Collectivization and new technology, however, are established everywhere, and universal education, the introduction of industry, state farming – which is farming carried out as an industry – and better communications are rapidly changing the lives of all Siberians. The ideas and ideology of socialism have had drastic effects on all native belief systems.

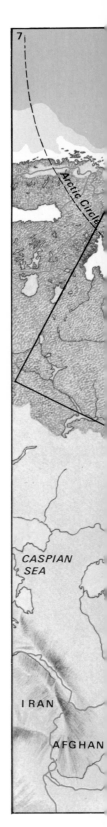

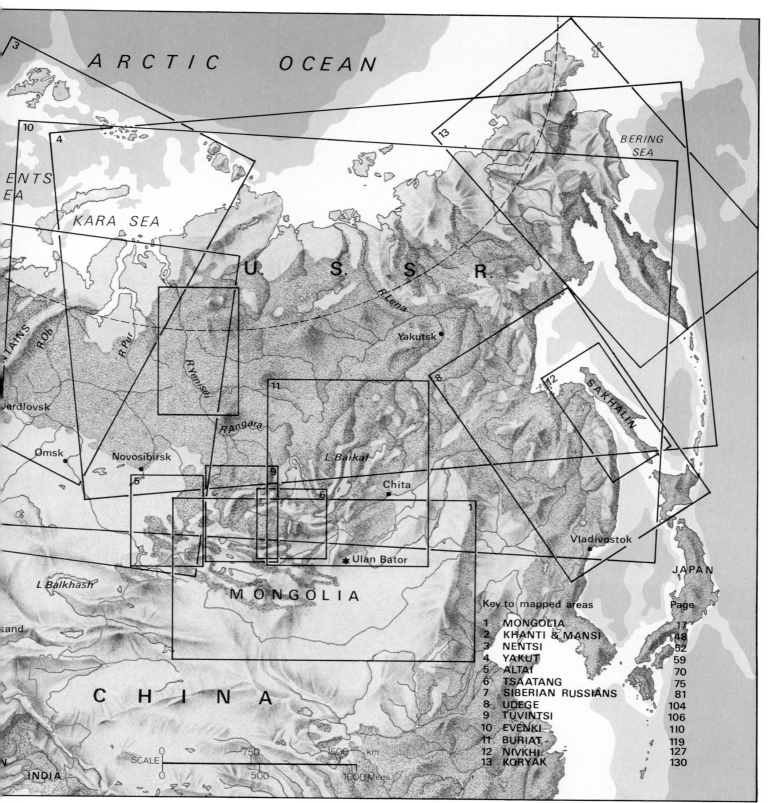

ARCTIC OCEAN

BERING SEA

ENTS EA

KARA SEA

U. S. S. R.

MOUNTAINS

R.Ob

R.Pur

R.Yenisei

R.Lena

Yakutsk

SAKHALIN

R.Angara

L.Baikal

verdlovsk

Omsk

Novosibirsk

Chita

Vladivostok

JAPAN

L Balkhash

Ulan Bator

MONGOLIA

kand

C H I N A

INDIA

Key to mapped areas	Page
1 MONGOLIA	17
2 KHANTI & MANSI	48
3 NENTSI	52
4 YAKUT	59
5 ALTAI	70
6 TSAATANG	75
7 SIBERIAN RUSSIANS	81
8 UDEGE	104
9 TUVINTSI	106
10 EVENKI	110
11 BURIAT	119
12 NIVKHI	127
13 KORYAK	130

SCALE

0   750   1500 km

0   500   1000 Miles

Peoples of Mongolia

A Mongolian writer, called Bansaraghi, once wrote of his country: 'He who knows our land little speaks of it as a land of endless steppe. However, steppe country in the literal sense of 'endless' does not occur there. The steppes here are huge spaces that lie between great mountain chains.' Mongolia is really a vast plateau covering 600,000 square miles, a land which averages some 4,000 feet above sea level. The eastern half is mainly plain, interrupted by mountains; the western half is mainly mountains, broken by plains.

Often the plainlands in Mongolia are surrounded by mountains as though in imitation of a bowl. From rim to rim the bowl may be 30 miles wide and between the mountains the grasslands rarely rise or dip. The floor is swept by cold winds, and except when heavy clouds burdened with snow gather from the north the sky radiates a clear blue. To every Mongol, Blue Sky is a holy phrase. Around the brooks and reedy lakes all kinds of small birds flourish, fluttering and singing in the clear light. Or a black stork may pause in the bulrushes, a hawk glide on the wind, a kite observe the world perched on a telegraph pole. Antelope graze on the plain, nervous of the slightest stirring; big bustards, birds bigger than geese, take to the air in convoys.

And then in the mountains there are the forests, towering cedars and tall larchs, firs and spruce and all kinds of shrubs bearing mountain fruit. Snakes bask in the sun among the rocks, and deer, elk and wolves range over all the slopes. Ermine, polecat, sable and marten yield their fur to hunters here in these mountains, and Mongol herdsmen boast that Mongolia has the most beasts in the world.

The southern third of Mongolia lies in the Gobi desert. But to the Mongols, Gobi is not a desert. It is not barren and lifeless except in places. The yellow color is not sand but a clay soil which supports yellow scrub. Although it will not feed cattle, it will keep camels going and sometimes even horses as well. The true desert of the Gobi begins only near the frontier, the bulk of it lying south of the border in China. Across here, for thousands of years, pilgrims, traders and missionaries have passed in caravan. Through Kansu, China's north-west, skirting Tibet and into Sinkiang, this route was called the Silk Route to Europe.

On the Mongolian plains the cold unceasing wind meets few trees or towns to curb its violence. The herdsmen say of the winds 'They dry the ponds, they blow the fish into the pasture.' Spring comes with deception, halting before a blizzard which blankets the ground in white. Only with the summer does the grassland become gay with sudden flowers, and bright with reds and yellows and blues. And then it is hot and men seek what shade they can find. At first the autumn is more pleasant, the nights become cool. But there are also sudden changes and snow may fall overnight to cover everything inches deep until, once again, the sun clears the gray sky and the

15

The nomad's herds are his life.
As the family roams
ceaselessly over the plains
children are brought up
astride their shaggy ponies.

Peoples of Mongolia

Red banners decorate Sukhe Bator Square in Mongolia's capital, Ulan Bator, in preparation for the National Day celebrations on 11 July.

Schoolchildren file through Ulan Bator. They wear gauze masks as a protection against infections like colds and influenza.

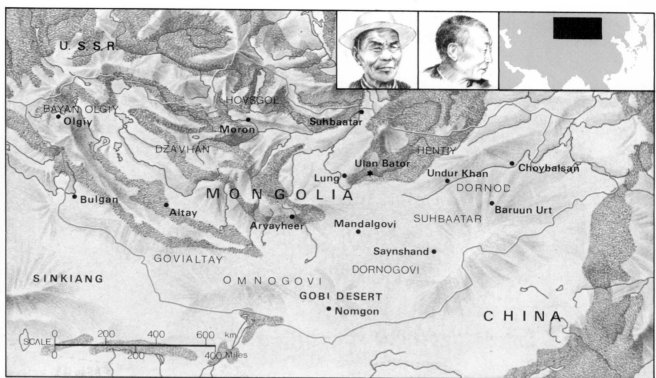

A statue of Mongolia's national hero Sukhe-Bator or Axe Hero rises above red and blue flags in the center of the square named after him.

(Over page) Waving red flags, the whole population of Ulan Bator crowds into Sukhe Bator square for the National Day celebrations.

Peoples of Mongolia

A woman walks past the Tchojin lama temple. When the baby on her back grows up the temple will be only a historic building in a new socialist state.

(Bottom) The lamas' absolute power kept Mongolia poor. In 1921 a third of all men were lamas supported by tributes from an already poor people.

ground becomes visible. Or there may be a downpour, and the brooks swell to rivers and courtyards vanish beneath a lake, With the winter the winds return and the temperature falls and falls until it has touched 40° or 50°F below zero and a man's breath hangs lifeless in the air.

The grassy plains and mountains of Mongolia are a stage between two extremes – to the north the Siberian taiga, those vast forested lands which reach a thousand miles beyond Lake Baikal to the tundra and frozen wastelands of the far north; and to the south the burning sands of central Asia. And in passing across these lands, you pass over untold layers of man's history and even beyond, to ages when dinosaurs roamed huge marshy fenlands which have now become the Gobi desert.

For thousands of years men have lived on these plains, huddled against the cold winds and snow, shading themselves from the heat. These men have been herders and nomads, hunters and horsemen. The men rode, the women rode, the children grew on horseback. Nomads, they followed their herds of cattle and yak, horses and flocks of sheep. They carried and pitched their tents, which they called *yurts,* wherever they went. They took

A lone member of Mongolia's decreasing number of monks kneels on a prayer board outside the temple at Gandan, Ulan Bator.

Lamas pray inside the temple at Gandan. They grow old and few of the young men come to learn from them, preferring to attend modern schools.

their food from their animals, they drank from their animals; they warmed themselves at fires which burned their animals' dung. They cultivated nothing, they settled nowhere. They fought with bow and arrow from horseback; they rallied to horse-tail banners; they wandered, they fought and they mixed.

Out of these early Mongolian tribes were soon to come waves of migrants, warriors and conquerors. They beat against the settled quarters of the world. By the 5th century AD, Mongolian tribes under Attila the Hun – the Scourge of God – threatened Rome. And in the 13th century, Genghis, the great khan, and his sons conquered the armies of civilizations from the Pacific to the Adriatic and for the first time brought the name Mongol to the lips of the world. His empire lasted 150 years and secured a place in the history of both Asia and Europe. But in Mongolia nothing of that epoch remains. It is almost forgotten, like the mounds of roughly-hewn black stones which in places rise out of the plain. They are memorials, so Mongol herdsmen explain. But to what, no-one remembers. Today few of the 900,000 people in Mongolia weep for the days of glory.

During the first thousand years BC, according to Chinese historians, there were three main groups of nomads. These were the Huns, ancestors of the present-day Turkic peoples of central Asia and Siberia; the Tung-hu, ancestors of the Mongols; and the Tung-i,

ancestors of the Tungus, Manchurians and ancient Asiatic peoples of north China and southern Siberia. By the 3rd century BC, the Huns were the strongest of these three groups. Based in a region which is now eastern Mongolia, about the Onon and Kerulen river valleys, the Huns even then dominated vast territories in central Asia and controlled the Silk Route from China to Europe.

In Mongolia, however, in 93 AD, the Huns were defeated by a union of Mongol-speaking tribes called Hsien-pi. But this union of tribes did not last long and it was not until the 6th century AD that a powerful and durable state emerged from the Asian steppe. This was the First Turkic Khanate which lasted for about 100 years. In the 7th century it was succeeded by a Second Khanate which was later, in 740 AD, overwhelmed by the Uighur, another Turkic people. During 200 years of Uighur rule, Buddhism, Manicheism and Nestorian Christianity spread through central Asia.

By the 10th century power on the central Asian steppe had passed back into the hands of Mongol-speaking peoples. The most important of these were the Khitan, descendants of the Hsien-pi tribes. They were more socially advanced than their predecessors. They were agriculturalists as well as nomadic herdsmen, they lived in houses not tents, and were competent at making salt, working in iron and weaving, pottery and other minor industries. The Khitan society already had a class 21

Peoples of Mongolia

One of the few Mongolian musical instruments is the violin. This has only two strings. Some have three or four and are richly carved and painted.

Built in 1912 and paid for by peasants, this gorgeous temple gate stands in the grounds of the Palace of the Living Buddha in Ulan Bator.

structure, headed by a feudal nobility, and a well-organized army. Their great leader was Elyui Ambagai (872–926) who conquered the whole of what is now Mongolia and built a series of garrison towns. Khitan agricultural techniques using irrigation spread as far west as the Altai, across Lake Baikal. In 947, the Khitan Empire, which included much of China, was called the Liao Dynasty and this lasted until 1125 when the Khitan were defeated by the Jurchen in alliance with the south China dynasty of Sung.

About this time the strictly Mongol tribes were also gaining strength. The Chinese called them Shivei. The Turks named them Tatar. At the beginning of the 13th century, Temujin, a son of the Borzhigin clan (which was related to the aristocracy of the Khitan), later to be known as Genghis Khan, united them into the alliance which was to create the vast Mongol Empire.

Genghis Khan attacked both Mongols and non-Mongols. If a tribe surrendered to his army without a struggle, he simply demanded certain duties and tributes and otherwise left them alone. If they resisted, they would be crushed, then divided up and transported in groups to

22

A demon looms menacingly from a temple wall: a work of art painstakingly painted by a long dead lama, who has lost his power now.

different parts of the Empire. In those early years, for the first time, groups of people with different ethnic origins and languages found themselves living in the same place. The administration was already beginning to be organized on a territorial basis, rather than by the traditional clan system.

Nevertheless the clans were still of fundamental importance to Mongol society. Each Mongol clan was allotted a territory and all inheritance rights to herding pastures and property came through the clan. Each clan had an allied group of other clans from whom its men took women as wives, and yet another group of clans to whom it gave sisters and daughters in marriage. The clan from which Genghis Khan came, the Borzhigin or Altan Urag (Golden Family), became the feudal aristocracy of old Mongolia. Each male member of the Golden Family was allotted a commoner clan which was expected to provide a certain number of soldiers. The commoners also had to perform feudal duties, like maintaining the post stations (which were among the most efficient in history), and supplying provisions. These services had to be maintained even in war, when the men of the families had gone off as soldiers. In many ways this system lasted unchanged until 1921.

Even during his lifetime Genghis Khan divided his territory between close members of his clan. His grandson Batu, for example, carved out an empire for himself in the west and came to head the great Golden Horde. His son Tului reigned in the east. His youngest brother headed the Mongols of the Upper Amur region, and so on. After his death, he was succeeded by his third son Ugedei. The capital of the Empire was then Karakorum, to the south-west of present-day Ulan-Bator. Many characteristic ways of the Mongols of those days can still be observed now: the *yurts,* their food and clothes. Even the traditional religion survived until quite recently.

After Genghis Khan's death in 1227, the Empire continued to grow. It reached central Europe in the west, Tibet and north India in the south, Korea in the east, the Yenisey in the north. But after the death of Ugedei there was to be continual dissension among the members of the Golden Family. Khubilai, younger grandson of Genghis Khan, conquered the powerful south Chinese Sung Dynasty, but he also had to deal with his younger brother Arig-Buga who had set himself up as emperor in Karakorum. Khubilai moved to China, received the Buddhist faith, and established Peking as his capital. He defeated Arig-Buga and in 1271 the Mongol Empire became the Yuan Dynasty. Yet Mongolia and the western parts of the Empire were still virtually independent, ruled by other sections of the Golden Family. The last Yuan Emperor was Togon-Temur, a weak victim of the vanities and excesses of Chinese civilization. In 1368 he was easily driven back to Mongolia by an anti-Mongol Chinese rebellion.

For 300 years after this Mongolia was torn by internal strife and the Empire gradually fell apart. The eastern Mongols, descendants of Togon-Temur, mostly Mongols of the Khalkha tribe, opposed the western Mongols, or Oirat. Later the eastern Mongols themselves split, the Khalkha opposing the southern Chakhar and Tumet.

In the 1630s the Manchu took advantage of this disarray. They allied themselves with the southern Mongols to defeat the Chinese and set up the Ch'ing Dynasty. The Khalkha, afraid of defeat at the hand of the Oirat, accepted Ch'ing suzerainty in 1691. This left only the Oirat or western Mongols free, and for 70 years they desperately fought the Manchu. Many migrated as far east as the Volga to find better pastures, a staggering journey for those days. Some remained there and are now called the Kalmuck Mongols. Another group, the Khoshut, made a migration almost as long, from the Altai to Tibet. But finally in 1756 the Oirat were defeated by the Manchu Ch'ing Dynasty armies. The Manchu were now undisputed rulers and divided Mongolia into two parts; Inner Mongolia (the part closer to China) and Outer Mongolia.

Manchu rule lasted from 1691 to 1911 and created the conditions which were later to lead many Mongolians to revolution. The people and land were divided into *khoshun,* ruled by princes who were mainly members of the Golden Family. The *khoshun* were grouped into leagues headed by the most senior lines of princes. These princes were given the title of khan and nominally supervised by Manchu officials living in settlements like Urga (now Ulan-Bator), Uliasutai and Kobdo. Mongol princes were given Manchu titles for their services to the emperor. Other princes who did not have *khoshun* of their own nevertheless had serf families who were duty-bound to help them with provisions and services. The ordinary Mongolian people, called the black ones, were not allowed to move outside the boundaries of their *khoshun* and had to provide the prince and his family with specific services. Only a few groups of people were exempt.

In the feudal Mongolian society, besides the lay feudal princes, there were also religious feudal lords. Buddhism had spread again over the Mongolian steppe in the 17th century. Encouraged by the Manchu, Buddhism was regarded as a way of turning the war-like Mongols to a peaceful passive way of life. Monasteries were built all over the country and allocated land and serfs. A monastery's territory was in some cases the administrative equivalent of the *khoshun,* but instead of being ruled by a prince, it was ruled by the head of the religious order – the lama. In other places monasteries were sited on land owned by princes, but a number of serfs and herds were privately owned by the religious lords – the Living Buddhas, reincarnations of deified holy men, like the Dalai Lama of Tibet. Hoping to gain religious merit, princes would give more and more of their serfs to the Living Buddhas. These serfs were called *shabinar.*

For the Mongolian commoners life still centered **23**

Peoples of Mongolia

Mongolia had no industries at the time of the Revolution, but since World War II light industry, especially textiles, has been developed.

(Center) Passers-by in Ulan Bator stop to read panels of news, propaganda and exhortations to the workers to increase production.

Each woman used to make felt boots for her own family. Now boot-making has become an industry and the women work in factories.

24

Few tourists visit Mongolia although a hotel has recently been built in Ulan Bator where guests' bills are reckoned with an abacus.

New apartment blocks spring up all over Mongolia, a country where, 20 years ago, everyone, even the wealthiest lords, lived in felt *yurts*.

around their herds of horses, cattle and sheep. Whatever the conditions, they were bound to give a certain proportion of their meat, wool and milk to the feudal lords. Although the lords were supposed to help their serf families in times of hardship, they too were hard hit by bad conditions. The serf family always had the worst of it. It was not rare to find a princely family reduced to complete poverty, and all its serfs gone. But at the same time other princes were extremely rich. They lived in luxury amid Chinese goods obtained by trade.

At this time in the Land of the Five Animals where most people were nomads, there were very few buildings apart from the lamaist monasteries. The few towns were almost invariably built around the walls of monasteries. Usually they consisted of administrative offices, stores and stables, Chinese trading-posts and a few houses or tents for visitors and dignitaries. Almost everyone, including the princes, lived in *yurts*, the felt tents which could be readily moved on to other pastures.

Most of the merchants in Mongolia were Chinese. They bought silks, tea, gunpowder, papers and many other things by camel caravan across the Gobi from China and sold them to the Mongol herdsmen. Often Mongols became dependent on things like flour, sugar and gunpowder yet were unable to pay the merchants.

The Chinese readily allowed credit but charged high interest rates. By the end of the 19th century Russian, Swedish and American traders had caught on and set up trade missions in Urga. But they never overtook the position of the Chinese. Besides trade, the Chinese in Mongolia did many kinds of work which the Mongols despised: carpentry, building, mending tools, water carrying and vegetable growing.

As an indication of the power the lamaist monasteries wielded in Mongolia, in 1921 monasteries owned one fifth of all the animal herds in Mongolia. Out of 300,000 men in Mongolia, an estimated 120,000 were lamas. The tradition was that every family should give one son (as long as there were two) to the local monastery to be a lama. The best-loved and most intelligent son was given as soon as he reached the age of about seven. Once inside the monastery, the boy had his hair shaved, wore a special robe and lived in a dormitory. Classes in reading Tibetan and Mongol prayers began immediately. There was a great deal of reading aloud in unison, learning by rote and chanting of Tibetan prayers whose meaning was sometimes not understood. This learning culminated in oral examinations which took the form of debates. After a few years if the boy was successful he could start studying more specialized subjects – mathematics, medi-

25

Peoples of Mongolia

The empire of Genghis Khan, the mighty ruler, stretched across all of Central Asia from the Pacific Ocean to the Black Sea.

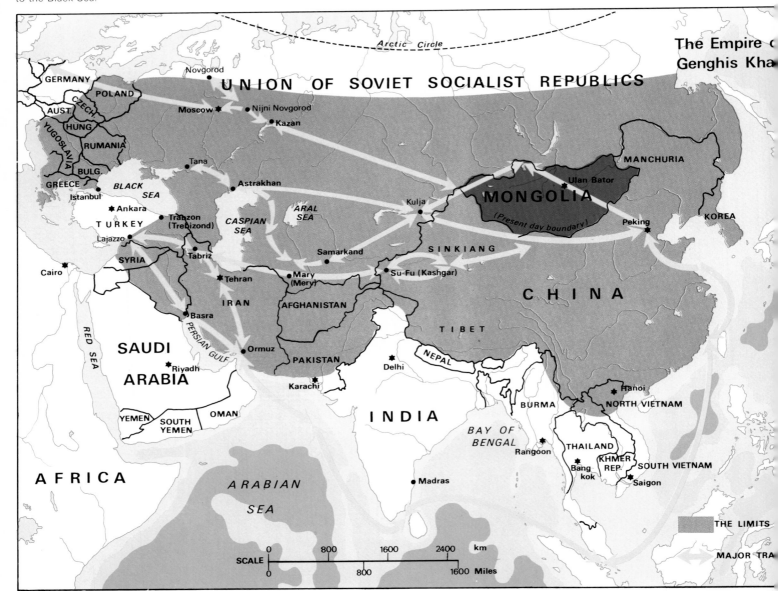

The Empire of Genghis Khan

The bow and arrow was always the Mongol's weapon both for war and for hunting. As a sport, archery is as popular as it ever was.

(Bottom) The bow is traditionally made from layers of wood, bone and horn covered in snakeskin. It used to be buried with its owner when he died.

Ever since the days of Genghis Khan the greatest honor a man could achieve was to win the wrestling championship and become an *arslan* or lion.

(Center) Wrestling is stylized. Contestants dance towards each other, flapping their arms. The winner of the bout must perform a victory 'eagle' dance.

cine, logic and astrology. Younger lamas were expected to serve older lamas throughout their youth. They made the tea, cooked, cleaned up the yard, herded the animals.

For the young lamas, life in a monastery very much depended on their family situation. If a boy came from a poor family, even if his parents had saved everything they could for him, he would have to take time off from his studies in order to earn his keep, either by becoming the servant of another lama or by doing small jobs. Sometimes these young lamas even had to leave the monastery to help their families over a difficult period. Some stayed away for years, taking a wife, having children and supporting the rest of the family. Such men only returned when they had no further responsibilities. Some lamas found that they could not support themselves in the monastery on public donations alone, and so they went out on long journeys, performing small rituals here and there, begging, collecting herbs for medicines and so on.

It was only the lamas with rich families (and those who were clever enough to cope with the rigorous education) who rose in the hierarchy, obtained degrees and titles and later became office-holders in the order. Mongolian lamas considered that the best education was

Genghis Khan in the 12th century united hundreds of tribes into one vast empire stretching across all central Asia from Europe to Korea.

to be obtained in Tibet. The most talented men would go there for several years learning esoteric Tantric formulas and practices. Others returned home with high degrees in one of the professions like medicine.

While there were many devout lamas there were, however, also others who took undue advantage of their position. They lived a self-indulgent life at the expense of the simple herders. Lamas were sometimes known to trick ordinary people. There are many stories of lamas pretending to chant prayers in the Tibetan language while in fact speaking of their devotees' possessions. 'Do you see his bull? Yes, it's a fat one. Let's get it off him. How? We'll say his son's dying . . .'

It was widely known that even some of the highest lamas disregarded their vows, drank alcohol and kept concubines. The very highest lama in the Mongol hierarchy, the Jebtsundamba Khutukhtu of Urga, even had a public concubine, euphemistically called his queen. It was argued, however, that since this lama was not only a holy reincarnation, a Living Buddha, and also the head of state, he was in fact two persons at once. And in his role of lay leader should be allowed to have a female companion. Yet to the ordinary, devout Mongol all this did not matter. What he worshipped was the spirit or deity successively reincarnated in the lamas: if one of the physical vessels of the deity was unworthy, it was a pity, but it did not affect the spiritual power inherent in the office of a Living Buddha.

Buddhism brought widespread literacy and learning to the Mongols. It also brought knowledge of the great Asian cultural traditions: painting, story-telling, music, drama, complicated ritual, theories about the nature of life, the human body, psychology and cosmology. In short, it was a universal system of beliefs and practices with an answer to almost any problem. Besides this, the church had a large and sophisticated hierarchical system which encompassed most of north Asia. In many matters it was more reliable and efficient than the state administration. And all of this was more impressive and powerful than the fragmented religious system of shamanism which had been the original religion of the Mongols. Lamaism answered to the needs of a population which itself had become hierarchical and feudal. Also there had always been some shamanistic elements in Tibetan lamaism – in trace-séances of *gurtumba* lamas for example. The Mongolian Buddhist church could in every way rival and outclass the old shamans. In the end only the outlying peoples of Mongolia remained shamanist by the beginning of the 20th century.

The monopolistic position of the lamaist church together with the selfish, backward-looking attitude of many of the feudal princes, resulted, however, in the eventual ruin of the primitive Mongolian economy. More and more riches were converted into money and consumer goods, and concentrated in the hands of high lamas, princes and merchants. The Chinese firm of

Nomads and warriors lived, slept and ate in the saddle. They even put meat under their saddles and rode until it was tender enough to eat.

(Bottom) So far, modernization has been achieved with the help of Russian and Chinese workers. Now Mongolians are taught to do the job themselves.

Ulan Bator is expanding rapidly. Mongolia's surge into the 20th century pushes her capital city into the foothills of the surrounding mountains.

Dashenku annually took 70,000 horses and 500,000 sheep in interest for debts from Mongolia. In 1911 Outer Mongolia was in debt to the tune of 11 million liang. The poorest Mongols were forced to near starvation. Many of them took to banditry as the only way of keeping alive.

Conservatism and some of the lamas' teachings – that it was a sin to till the earth – kept the Mongols from turning to agriculture as a new means of subsistence. The large number of lamas, who were thought to lose religious merit if they engaged in manual labor, was a further drain on the economy. The 1905 rebellion in Russia spread to Mongolia. A herdsman called Ayush led a rising against the feudal administration. He demanded the lessening of post-messenger service duties, freedom from feudal taxes, changes in the privileges of the princes and cancellation of debts to Chinese merchants. The uprising was defeated by the Manchu-Chinese army.

The fall of the Manchu Ch'ing Dynasty in 1911 was seized upon by the Mongols as a real chance of freedom. All Mongols, rich and poor, were now united against the hated Chinese. The Manchu administrators were driven out of Urga with little trouble and a committee of princes and high lamas declared Mongolia autonomous. The

A shiny red motor bike has replaced the horse for one Mongol at least, but he still lives in the traditional circular felt *yurt*.

(Bottom) Some say that the Mongols invented the saddle. Whether true or not, they were certainly one of the earliest peoples to tame horses.

new state was headed by the only man to have acknowledged power over everyone: the High Lama, Jebstsundamba Khutukhtu of Urga, who was given the title Bogdo Gegeen. But Autonomous Mongolia extended only over Outer Mongolia, not over Inner Mongolia. And the new government agreed, in return for recognition by China, to leave foreign and economic policy in the hands of the Chinese.

The government of Autonomous Mongolia proposed a number of reforms and in a vague way also aimed at a united Mongolia, which would include Inner Mongolia. But none of their plans really came to anything. In 1919 they were alarmed, rather than delighted, at the attempt of Ataman Semenov, anti-revolutionary ally of the White Guards in Siberia and the Japanese, to create a Great Mongolian State, stretching from Lake Baikal to Tibet. Then, at the end of 1919, Urga was captured by a Chinese war-lord, nicknamed Little Hsu, who forced the Mongol government to sign a petition renouncing autonomy. It was during the two years of Hsu's occupation, universally disliked by the Mongols, that revolutionary organizations were set up in Urga by young Mongols. The most notable was called Sukhe-Bator or Axe Hero. When in 1921 Hsu was ousted by the White Guard leader, Baron von Ungern-Sternberg, whose rule was unbearably capricious and cruel, these organizations took an active part in opposing his army.

The Mongolian People's Revolutionary Party had its first congress at Maimachen on the Siberian-Mongol border in March 1921. Some of the leaders of the party had been trained in Russian communist institutions in Irkutsk. A temporary People's Government was appointed, and it was decided that the first priority was to remove von Ungern-Sternberg from Urga. The Mongol Revolutionary Army was very small at this time, and appealed to the Red Army for help. Since von Ungern-Sternberg was an enemy of the Russians as well, the Red Army agreed. By May 1921 the Mongol and Russian revolutionaries, lead by Sukhe-Bator, had taken Urga.

It now had to be decided what form the new government of Mongolia would take. The lamaist church was still strong and so were the feudal princes. Many of them had even supported the Revolutionary Army's attack on the White Guards. The new government decided not to destroy the old order immediately. The High Lama, Bogdo Gegeen, remained as head of state and the princes kept their administrative roles. However a number of important steps were taken to alter Mongol society forever. Land became state-owned. Debts to foreigners were annulled. Feudal dues were abolished. Princes and other feudal dignitaries were made to pay taxes and allowed only the same pasture rights as other Mongols. The lamas could no longer legally extract payments for religious services. A state trading company was set up.

When, in 1924, the Bogdo Gegeen died, Mongolia was proclaimed a Republic. The highest organ of govern-

A woman milks one of 400 horses on the Tuya collective farm. Her husband holds the foal close by to encourage the mare to give plenty of milk.

ment was now to be the Great Hural, the National Congress, though policies and decisions were carried out by committees on the Soviet model. The lamas began their usual procedure for finding a new reincarnation of the Jebtsundamba Khutukhtu, but in the end their attempts were blocked; a new reincarnation was never appointed. Through the 1920s the whole of the old social order in Mongolia was gradually changed. But it was not until the 1940s that the Mongolian government felt free of serious internal dissension. The monasteries were disbanded in the late 1930s and many of the lamas returned to ordinary lay lives. But thousands resisted the changes in Mongol society and were savagely punished for it. It is likely that repression took place in Mongolia on the Soviet model. By the 1940s there were no feudal princes, no serfs, no *khoshuns,* virtually no monasteries, no *shabinar* (serfs) and no foreign traders. The country was beginning to develop on completely new lines, leaping from feudalism straight towards socialism.

Politically and socially the Land of the Five Animals was no longer the same country. And yet there were many aspects of Mongolian life that could not be altered. The most ancient sources told that Mongolians had always based their economy on herding horses, sheep, cattle and yaks, goats and camels, and traditional herding techniques, adapted to the conditions of their harsh

31

Grandmother samples a glass of the Mongol's favorite summer drink, *kumiss,* fermented mare's milk. Fresh milk is rarely drunk. Every drop is saved for *kumiss.*

Herds of wild horses roam the steppe following the nomads. Specially trained, easily caught, catcher horses run with the herd until they are needed.

(Bottom) The catcher horse has been trained to chase its quarry like a hound while the rider drops his reins and uses his hands for the lasso.

steppeland, were as valuable to the new Mongolia. The cold mountain forests and dry, flat plains of Mongolia demand different techniques of herding. The length of herding journeys differs according to the availability of water and grass. It was traditional to move four times a year, from winter to spring pastures, from spring to summer pastures, from summer to autumn, and from autumn back to winter pastures. The most permanent of these were the winter pastures and the winter camp. The herdsmen and their families tended to return here year after year, to the same corrals and sheds built long before. In some parts, like the grassy Khangai region, it was only necessary to move a short distance from winter pastures in the hills, to summer pastures in the valleys; but in the dry eastern steppe herders might have to move up to 30 miles from camp to camp, going from summer pastures in low places near water sources to winter pastures on the sunny slopes of hills with no snow. In the far west of Mongolia herders spent the summer in the high pastures which were snow and ice-covered at other times in the year, then descended in winter to the lower, more sheltered slopes. In the southern Khangai people spent the summer in the low hills, the winter in the lower, snowless parts of the Gobi.

Traditionally the Mongols did not prepare hay to feed their herds in winter, nor did they cultivate any other fodder; they only constructed shelters for the very young animals against the cold and predators. No special fields of rich grass were irrigated or manured. The Mongols were therefore forced to keep their herds on the move if they were to stay alive. For the sheep, goats, cattle and camels the herders had to look for dry, snowless places in winter. Horses, on the other hand, could dig grass out even from hard snow-cover. Yaks required high, fairly moist conditions and could withstand great cold. Goats, vulnerable to cold, could live in very dry conditions during the spring and summer. Each animal in Mongolia had its special needs and preferences.

Every herding family ideally had herds of each of the five animals. But co-operation evolved to deal with the inevitable difficulties. In a particular valley the son of one family would herd everyone's horses on a distant pasture, while the daughter of another family might look after all the goats. It was common for the cows belonging to several families to be taken out to graze in one herd, although they were milked separately, morning and evenings, by each housewife. Sometimes two small families, not necessarily related, would go everywhere together, for several years helping one another, although maintaining their independence.

The worst disasters in the annual cycle were drought in spring or summer and the *zud* in winter. There were several kinds of *zud*. Black *zud* happened when not enough snow fell in winter and thousands of animals died because the grass did not appear in spring. White *zud* was the case when there was too much snow and ice in winter,

and the animals died of exposure and lack of nourishment. Hoof *zud* was when the herds trampled a small pasture so much that the grass did not grow properly and the animals died of starvation. Spring in Mongolia was always dry, but a drought at this time made the grass wiry and thin and insufficiently nourishing to prepare the herds for the rigors of the following winter. Besides these disasters, winter storms and long cold spells would kill many animals. The colder the winter, the more likely were wolves or other predators to attack the flocks. In summer it was not rare for lightning to strike herders or animals in the exposed steppe. Cattle diseases and epidemics regularly carried off many animals from the herd.

A disaster seldom hit all kinds of animals equally, but it was always easier for the herdsman to re-build his flock, than it would have been for a farmer to re-establish fields baked by drought or silted over by a flood. This was the real advantage of the nomadic herdsmen over the peasant farmers. In the past in Mongolia this advantage was, however, tempered by the feudal system which tied people to particular monasteries or princes, and by the recalcitrant lamas who forbade vaccination even in the

Kicking and bucking, the wild horse often forces the man to dismount and be dragged along using his boots like skis until, exhausted, it stands quiet.

(Bottom) Men gather round to hold the wild horse and to saddle and bridle it. Then, for the first time, the horse feels the weight of its new rider.

Catching and breaking in wild
horses is the nomad's life and
his greatest joy. His songs are
more often about his horses
than about women or love.

1926 disaster when in one district three out of four cows
died within a few weeks.

Of course the Mongol herdsmen did not suffer these
misfortunes entirely passively. They had a variety of
remedies. Medical treatment for animals included sur-
gery, acupuncture, poultices and herbal mixtures, as well
as magical rites. To combat drought the herdsmen
assessed the best routes and pastures, and performed
magical rain-making ceremonies. These ceremonies go
far back in central Asian history to the Turkic tribes who
were neighbors of the ancient Mongols. These were even
used by the Mongols of the early feudal period as a
military device. The son of Togon-Temur, last of the
Yuan Emperors, used a rain-making ceremony as he was
fleeing from China: he raised a great blizzard in which
most of his enemy's men and horses were frozen to death.
The survivors, fleeing back to China and the Great Wall,
dug holes in the steppe such as the Mongols use as stoves
when the wind prevents making a fire on the surface;
they even burnt their spears in a vain endeavor to keep
warm, and then died of exposure, crouched in the 'fire-
holes'. This same rain-magic was used comparatively
recently by the Buriat Mongols in the USSR and the
Ordos Mongols in China. Traditionally, however, there
were restrictions on the practice of rain-making: the art
should never be practised in winter, for fear of harming
plants and animals, which would be a criminal act;
neither should it be performed frequently in summer,
since this would encourage swarms of worms and insects.
The ceremony among the Ordos Mongols went as
follows. The lamas, who were asked to 'invite' the rain,
went to swampy ground. They dug down until they
reached water, and, having previously poured a little
water in an earthenware bottle, they put the rain-stone in
it and placed the bottle in the little well. The rain-stone
magically attracted rain. It was white, round and about
the size of a pheasant's egg. The lamas prayed over the
bottle in the well for three days, and the people who
invited them abstained from smoking, drinking spirits
and eating meat during this period. There is historical
evidence that virtually the same ceremony with the rain-
stone was performed in ancient times by shamans.

The family of a Mongolian herdsman was called orkh,
which literally means 'the square felt cover of the yurt's
smoke hole'. Usually these nomads lived in small camps
of two or three yurts. A rich man's tent might be about 20
feet in diameter and 10 feet high in the center. A poor
man's tent would be smaller. In a camp all the tents were
put with their doors to the south and the most senior
man placed his tent to the right of the others. It was
common for a family to have aged parents living with
them, or other dependent relatives, widowed aunts and
uncles, unmarried sisters, orphaned children. A rich
family sometimes camped together with a serf family.
Sometimes two married brothers would camp together
for a while for, although the simple family was the basic

The short, stocky horse with its long mane and tail can gallop all day. No other animal could have carried Genghis Khan to victory across the vast steppe.

Peoples of Mongolia

An old man roams the steppe with his herd of sheep and goats. They, too, are valued like the horse in the 'Land of the Five Animals'.

Felt is made from goat and sheep's wool. The goat is caught and tied then the herdsman combs through its long thick coat.

Making felt is an important part of the women's work. As many as six or even eight layers of felt will cover the *yurt* in winter.

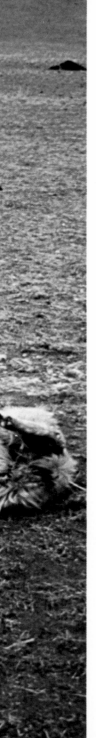

economic unit, it was always more convenient to live and herd in co-operation with a number of other people. Children were useful in herding from an early age, and it was common for a family with many children to give a son or daughter in adoption to a close relative with few children. Even if children were not formally adopted they often went away for long periods to stay with relatives. The tightly knit, private nuclear family did not exist.

The *yurt* was built of wooden lattice walls joined with thongs of camel leather. The lattices folded up for traveling. A small tent had four walls, a large one six or more. About forty wooden poles connected the top of the lattices with a circular wooden wheel-like structure which, held up by two posts stuck into the ground, supported the roof. The center of the wheel was left open, as a smoke-hole. This whole framework was covered with layers of felt. Nowadays there is an outside cover made of waterproof canvas.

Immediately inside the door of a Mongol tent was a square wooden box containing dried dung for fuel. Just behind it in the center of the tent was the fireplace, a hearth dug into the ground and a metal brazier over which the cooking-pot was suspended. Today there is a metal stove instead of the brazier. The advantage of this is that it contains the ashes, and the smoke goes through a metal chimney, instead of lingering in the tent.

All the other furniture was ranged round the walls. On the left as one entered was the male side. Here, immediately by the door was a very large leather bag supported on a crossbeam from two posts. This was the bag in which mare's milk was fermented to make *kumiss*, the favorite summer drink of the Mongols. It was considered polite for junior visitors and children to churn their hosts' *kumiss* one hundred times as a sign of thanks. Further along this west wall were the saddle, bridle, whip, gun and axe of the master of the household. All were hung up so that they did not touch the floor. Next there was sometimes a large wooden chest, or a bed on top of a chest of drawers. These old chests were beautifully painted with traditional designs of lions, bears and other animals and flowers. Directly opposite the door, against the northern wall, was the altar. There was a little table covered with silk cloths and small bowls, lamps, statues of Buddha and prayer-wheels. Today these religious images have been replaced by paintings and photographs of heroes, famous men and family members. A box containing precious or ancient objects will also be placed in this position.

In the female half of the tent there was another chest, exactly like the first one, containing the wife's clothes and possessions. Next was the marital bed, if the family was rich enough to own a bed. Then there were the tools for cleaning and tanning leather, for sewing and felt-making, and for all the other women's jobs. Lastly, by the door, there was a wooden cupboard for the iron cooking pots, the wooden milk pails and all cooking things. Stores of dried cheese, curds, flour, salt and dried meat and herbs were also hung up in skin bags in this cupboard.

On the floor of the *yurt* skins and felt mats were laid. The simple white felt mats were sewn with intricate patterns. The family sat either on the mats, or on tiny wooden stools. The host usually sat opposite the door and important male guests sat to his right in the men's half. Less important men sat nearer the door. Women and children always kept to the left of the host.

A man usually had only one wife, though he could have two, or even three, if the first did not give him children. It was also possible for a man to take a concubine. Marriage was usually arranged by the parents, many years in advance of the actual wedding. And the whole procedure was governed by strict conventions. A match-maker from the groom's side would arrive at the tent of the chosen bride's father. The match-maker had to be both a respected man, and a persuasive speaker. After certain polite preliminaries he would make his proposal, describing the bride-groom's family in the most flattering terms. If the bride's parents intended to accept they invited him in and prepared a dinner in his honor. In some districts families killed a sheep specially for a match-maker and placed before him the most honored portion: the head. Small ritually prescribed bits of meat were eaten from different parts of the head before the guest could move on to more substantial meat. Sometimes the groom's father was also present at this meal and the prospective marriage was symbolized in some regions by the two fathers exchanging silk belts. A most important part of this betrothal procedure was the settling of the size and content of the bride-price. This was the number of horses which the groom's family promised to pay on marriage. By tradition they should have paid nine horses or multiples of nine, but a poor family would substitute other animals for horses. It was not possible to give a bride-price in money alone. The very poorest family gave at least a dressed sheep, of which the liver, symbolizing

37

Peoples of Mongolia

Although Mongolia is extremely cold in winter, snow does not often lie thickly. Strong winds sweeping across the steppe quickly blow it away.

(Bottom) The *stupas* of 16th century Erdeni Dzuu monastry rise above the snow. Formerly 1,000 lamas lived here, now only a few remain as caretakers.

kinship, had to be in perfect condition.

Opinions always differed as to which girls would make the best wives: some thought that a quiet, hard-working girl was best; others preferred a girl who already had a baby. The slight scandal of a child born out of wedlock was unimportant compared with the knowledge that she was not barren. In some parts of Mongolia the bride and the groom did not see each other until the ceremony itself. But in central Mongolia the boy usually paid a visit to the girl's family, taking seven kinds of special presents: a ceremonial silk scarf for each of the girl's parents, milk wine, cheese, glue, soft, tough animal skin, a file and offerings for the altar in the girl's tent. The boy placed butter as a sacrificial offering on the fire, and a speaker who had come with him explained the meaning of the gifts: the glue was meant to stick the couple together, the leather to bind them together and the file to remove the hard edges. The third phase of the marriage consisted of transferring the bride-price to the girl's family. Then, allowing a sufficient time for the girl's family to make their wedding preparations, came the final phase: a feast and a ceremony at the girl's camp.

After the birth-dates of both bride and groom were reckoned an auspicious day was selected by the lamas.

38

(Right) Occasionally the wind blows the sands of the Gobi into fantastic rolling dunes, but most of the Gobi is clay covered with yellow scrub.

Peoples of Mongolia

The two-humped bactrian camel is the Mongol's principal beast of burden. Lines of camels pull two-wheeled wooden carts laden with hay.

Camels are loaded with household goods when the nomads move camp. Caravans carry salt from remote salt lakes in the mountains.

On very long journeys in great cold camels are better than horses. Their coats are thicker and they travel for two weeks without food or water.

A family blessed with many children often sent a son or daughter to live with childless relatives and help them with their herds.

The boy and his family arrived at the girl's camp bringing the new *yurt* with them. The bridal party took place in the girl's father's tent, where ceremonial presents were given by each side and the bride and groom were required to bow deeply to all their senior relatives. Then the bride and groom entered their tent for the first time. The girl undid her single plait of hair and re-plaited it into two pig-tails; she also took off the silk belt she had worn as a girl – both of these acts signified that she was now a married woman. Inside the *yurt* the couple performed another simple ceremony. They were given two small brass cups without stems, the bases of which were connected with a red cord. The boy's cup contained milk wine, the girl's contained milk. Each partner held the cup in a silk scarf, and they simultaneously drank half of the contents of their cups. Then they exchanged cups and drained them. Only after all these ceremonies and the feast of the wedding, could the couple spend their first night together. A special bed was made for them on the right side of the *yurt*. *Bergen*, older women married into the bride's or groom's families, who took on the role of jesters at the wedding, also shared the *yurt* on this night. They slept on the left side of the tent and were supposed to undress the bride, prevent her escaping and joke away all her fears.

The wedding was then over and the couple went to live near the boy's father. Already they were economically independent, since it was customary for a son to take a share of his father's herds. The girl was entitled to a dowry from her father and, after a decent interval had elapsed, she would go home to collect it. The animals in the dowry were joined to her husband's herds. If she and her husband fell on hard times, she could go home several times for more animals. These animals remained hers in theory and she could take them with her if she and her husband were divorced. The woman's status among the Mongols was not as low as among many herding peoples. Sometimes the wife was richer than her husband. When a man had an only daughter, instead of sending her away to get married and letting a brother or nephew inherit his property, he might allow his daughter to inherit, bringing a son-in-law to live with her. The property would then pass to the daughter's sons. This kind of marriage was considered a disgrace for a man, but it was fairly common because high bride-prices made it difficult for poor men to get married at all.

In winter the staple diet of the Mongols was mutton, particularly fatty mutton. A sheep would always be meticulously butchered without letting the blood escape and without cutting the bones. The head, the breast and the tail fat were thought the best parts. They also ate beef, yak and goat meat and sometimes horse or camel meat. Often, in winter, meals were supplemented with deer, gopher, bear or squirrel. But there were also many foods the Mongols would not touch: fish, chicken, pork, eggs, most vegetables and the meat of wild birds.

In the summer Mongol nomads lived almost entirely on milk products like cheese, curds, yoghurt, buttermilk, clarified butter and clotted creams. For everything except *kumiss*, yak's milk was considered the best while camel and goat's milk was the worst. Mare's milk was almost never drunk fresh: every drop was conserved to make *kumiss*. Various alcoholic drinks were made from milk. The most common was made by boiling yoghurt and draining off the liquid forming on the roof of the pan.

The Mongols lived almost entirely off their herds. By rejecting other foods like cultivated vegetables and animals, like pigs and hens, which needed sheds, they kept themselves free to move anywhere at any time. It was this freedom, of which they were very proud, that not only made the mixed herding economy viable but also gave the Mongols a distinct military advantage in both attack and withdrawal. The Mongol nomads say: 'If you eat grass you become like a cow; if you eat meat, you become like a wolf.'

For Mongol men there were three traditional sports – the three men's contests – which took up much of their time away from the herds. Horse-racing was the first. The feudal traditional post-horse routes covering thousands of miles made the Mongols more interested in stamina than in short bursts of speed. Races were run over distances of 20 to 30 miles at a straight gallop. The jockeys were young children, both boys and girls, up to 41

On her wedding night a Mongol
girl unties her single plait
of hair and replaits it into
two braids signifying her
new married status.

the age of about eight. Many men bred and trained race-horses with a passionate interest. And this is a sport which is still as popular today. In recent years the most important race has been the open race held at the *naadam* festival which falls in July at Ulan-Bator. But there are other small *naadams*, and races are held all over the country during the summer.

The second traditional Mongol sport is wrestling. A wrestler wins if any part of his opponent's body touches the ground. There are no weight restrictions and it is said that the smaller man often has an advantage in keeping his balance over the larger man. Mongol wrestling is rather formalized. The winner performs a victory dance, waving his arms like a flying bird. Wrestlers are graded according to their achievements in the national championships. The best are called lions, the next best elephants and so on; hawk is the lowest grade.

The third of these traditional sports is archery. The bow and arrow were formerly the Mongol's weapon in both war and hunting. According to the traditions, the bow is made in layers of wood, bone and horn covered with snakeskin, with a hand-grip of soft leather. The string is made from one long strip of leather. The bow has always been treated with great respect; it was given a speech of praise and a libation of *kumiss* before it was first used, and never allowed to touch the ground. The bow, placed by his right hand, even accompanied its owner to the grave.

At an archery contest the archer stands 70 or 75 yards from the target and clasps the bowstring between thumb and index finger. He draws the arrow back horizontally, then suddenly turns it upwards to shoot. The judges stand next to the target and indicate a hit by raising their arms in the air. Throughout the shooting they call out ritual words: the invitation words, when the arrow begins its flight; the joyful words, when the arrow attains its goal; the examination words, when the points are counted up. Even the arrow has been symbolically important in Mongol culture. The word *sum* was used both for an arrow, and for the smallest feudal unit of soldiers, for the side seam of the Mongol gown and for the central thong of the horse's hobble.

Horse-racing, wrestling, archery, these are timeless things, like the herds which still roam the plains and steppe. But Mongolia has also had a revolution. A completely new government policy has been created. Improving productivity in the country's economy has meant giving direct aid to herdsmen – veterinary services, winter fodder and shelters for the animals, facilities for cross-breeding with better strains of animals. There are more domestic animals per head of population in Mongolia than in any other part of the world. Without feudal lords, owning all and giving little in return, the new government gradually persuaded Mongol herdsmen to relinquish private ownership of their herds.

The first experimental communes were called *khoton*.

Fish is a rare and welcome addition to the diet. A fisherman from the commune on lake Hövsgöl Nuur rows out to check the nets.

These were co-operatives for herding, preparing hay, building the winter shelters, digging wells – but at this stage the animals were still privately owned. In the 1930s the government confiscated the herds of rich princes and lamas. Then, through the 1940s and 1950s, the communes grew in strength and full collectivization and co-operative ownership of the herds were introduced in the 1960s. Virtually all herdsmen now belong to a co-operative or *negdel*.

In the *negdel* each family has its own (privately owned) *yurt* or house, and also between 50 and 70 animals. There are buildings for a school, a meeting house, a club, a clinic, and here the elected head of the *negdel* and his committee administer the co-operative. Most of the men spend their time with the herds, but the economy is also more diverse and *negdel* members produce hay, some crops and vegetables. There is mechanization and all *negdels* now have sheep-shearing machines; many also have mechanized milking. There are plans to bring water to the pastures used by the herders and Soviet and Mongolian specialists investigate underground water sources. It was aimed to have 1,500 wells in the country by the end of the third Five Year Plan and this should water 40,000 acres of land.

Since World War II Mongolia has been developing industry as well as its agriculture. Electricity brings power, coal is mined, timber is felled, cement, bricks and ferro-concrete are produced. Light industries manufacture textiles, felt, leather footwear, leather coats, carpets. Meat, milk, butter, flour, bread, spirits and beer emerge from factories. A modern city called Darkhan, with factories and blocks of flats, has been built with the help of Soviet and East European technicians to rival Ulan-Bator as the industrial center. Education has brought literacy close to 100 per cent; there are compulsory schools for children between the ages of eight and fifteen. A university in Ulan-Bator teaches physicists and mathematicians, engineers and social scientists; other colleges teach economics, medicine, agriculture, education and physical culture. The first hospital was built in Mongolia in 1926 and since then the number has been steadily increasing. There is now one medical specialist to every 714 Mongolians and diseases like plague, tuberculosis and venereal disease have been brought under control.

Today in Mongolia many people live in flats and houses in the towns, and no longer in *yurts*. They turn on electricity and gas, warm themselves with central heating. In the towns there are parks and cinemas, theaters, museums and exhibition halls. The country is full of contrasts. Side by side with the modern ways is the timeless herding culture. Mongolians still move with the needs of their flocks and herds, sit by a dung fire to hear the ancient epics sung to the horse-fiddle, and reckon the time by the angle of the shaft of sunlight which enters their tent by the smoke-hole.

The fish freeze quickly in the cold air. They can be left piled in a hut until a truck arrives to take them to Ulan Bator, about 500 miles away.

43

Shamanism

The icy Siberian wind moans and howls across a barren wasteland cloaked in the shadow of the long Arctic night. Inside a small crude hut the men and women of a small isolated community sit in silence. One man, the shaman, stands in the center. He begins to beat a drum. The monotonous drum beats go on and on and gradually the shaman enters a frenzied trance. He appears to lose control of his actions, he jumps and dances around. He shouts commands to things unseen and strange voices reply above the shrieking wind. The shaman's helper spirits have entered his body, they have come to guide his soul into another world. He falls as if unconscious to the ground. The people wait, for they know that the shaman has sent his soul into the other world to do battle on their behalf. They hope that when he returns he will be able to tell them why the hunting has been bad, why the fish seem to have disappeared from the sea or why a man lies sick. He will tell them where the herds of deer have gone, which taboos they have broken, which spirits they have offended. With the shaman's help the sick and the hungry will live through the long winter.

Life was a hard and bitter struggle for these people of the tundra, the marsh and the taiga. Their survival de-

pended on the maintenance of a very delicate balance of forces natural and unnatural. These forces could be upset and the whole community plunged into danger by the slightest deviation. For instance, if the deer changed their migration routes and the hunters were unable to kill a winter's supply, their families would starve before spring. Every community had a shaman who used his knowledge and skills and the help of friendly spirits to enter a trance and send his soul into the spirit world for the well-being of the community. It was a dangerous task, for the shaman had somehow to achieve an ecstatic trance state without losing control and descending into madness. Shamans reached a trance in various ways – some by monotonous drumming or chanting; some took the hallucinogenic mushroom, fly agaric. This is the red-capped fungus flecked with white which is so common in European fairy tales. Fly agaric grows in the temperate forest regions and was highly valued by the Siberian peoples especially the Tungus, Yakut, Chukchi, Koryak and also the Finno-Ugrian peoples the Khanti, Ket and Mansi. In 1870, a traveler who visited the Chukchi reported that they traded three or four reindeer for a single mushroom.

But whichever method he used to reach a trance, every

A modern-day shaman uses the fishbone rattle and moosehide drum to attain the desired communication with the spirits.

The shaman's drum is the instrument through which his helper spirits guide him into the other world to fight evil on behalf of the whole tribe.

(Bottom) The special mirror is used to light the shaman's way in the spirit world, to capture souls and to shield him against evil spirits.

shaman had a drum which was often painted with the figures of reindeer or his animal helping spirit. Many shamans also had a mirror through which they could see into the future. Helping spirits usually appeared in the form of animals – bears, dogs, snakes, birds, reindeer or fish. Sometimes they were the spirits of ancestors or other shamans.

For hundreds of years, some scholars say for thousands, shamanism spread across the lands of the far north: the Arctic tundra, the forests of the sub-Arctic taiga, and the steppes lying to the south.

In the Arctic region life was at its hardest and most primitive. People lived in small family or tribal groups separated by long distances from their clansmen. In this harsh land men and women, who were very often short of food and always exposed to the elements, frequently suffered from uncertainty and nervous diseases, such as hysteria, spirit possession and coprolalia (obsessive use of obscene language). In these communities every family had its shaman, usually a man. He was not a tribal leader or clan chief but a man born to his craft and called by the spirits. Because he was possessed by his spirits he usually needed to take less hallucinogenic mushrooms than the rest of the community to induce a trance. Shaman séances were violent and the shaman often showed signs of sexual neuroses. But when not called upon to enter the spirit world the shaman, of necessity, did his share of work in the tribe.

There were differences between the shamanism of the eastern and western Arctic peoples. In the east, on the Kamchatka peninsula, the most ancient form of shamanism was preserved among the primitive Koryak tribe. Shamans were graded according to their performance: how they reached a trance, what journeys their spirits took, what they tried to accomplish – curing the sick, remembering or guiding the souls of the dead. The western peoples, like the Nentsi who live between the rivers Ob' and Yenisei, graded their shamans by their equipment which also determined their level of learning. The apprentice shaman was given a drumstick. Later he earned a drum and special clothing. Finally he was accorded special headgear making him a fully-fledged shaman.

In the sub-Arctic region, between the 60th and 45th parallels, the people were forest hunters. They were also able to keep reindeer and horses. Family groups hunted and herded separately and their shamans worked on behalf of the tribe. Life was slightly easier and fewer people suffered from Arctic hysteria. To induce a trance the shamans took mushrooms. Many of the more nervous and impressionable women also became shamans. But men had to complete an apprenticeship to an experienced shaman. Shamans established a sexual contact with their helping spirits. In some families of the tribe shamanism became an hereditary occupation.

In this sub-Arctic region live the Ugrians and Tungus

45

(Evenki, pages 110-117). These people moved to the north from the southern steppes where they bred animals. Their shaman séances were rich in poetry, part of a whole wealth of archaic drama and customs mixed with legends. Further east, in the Altai-Sayan region, live the Buriat and some Turkish clans. Their shamanism was influenced by southern, principally Tibetan, culture.

The people who lived in the far eastern sub-Arctic region, along the Amur river and on the island of Sakhalin formed a different group. Their shamanism was extremely primitive and linked to tribal cults. This was probably due to their settled way of life which led them to develop a different social structure to the other Arctic peoples who were all nomadic or semi-nomadic. Generally the shamanism of the sub-Arctic peoples varied according to the number of helping spirits invoked and what the shaman tried to achieve through his craft.

Only in its southernmost region, in the steppes, the transitional territory of shamanism, did shamanism develop into a fully fledged religion. The people who live on these grassy plains, the European Finnish Ugrians, the Mongols, Manchurians, Kazakh, Kirghiz and other Central Asian Turkish tribes were herders and primitive farmers. Their social structure was based on clans and clan alliances which finally formed the state. Their shamans had the status of professional priests. However this situation occurred only occasionally, at the height of social development, during the time of the great nomadic empires which quickly grew powerful, but equally quickly disintegrated.

Animism and ancestor worship preceded shamanism in the steppes. Traces of these early religions can still be found among the Mongol and Turkish peoples. There has been much scholarly debate about the relation of animism and ancestor worship to shamanism and about the origin of shamanism. Some scholars, relying on linguistic evidence, have tried to prove that itinerant Buddhist missionaries first developed shamanism into a religion. The word shaman seems to support this theory. It is believed to come from the Sanskrit Pali *sramana* which means itinerant 'Buddhist monk'. But it is far more difficult to discover when shamanism reached the steppes. The Mongols were shamanists at the time of Genghis Khan. In the 13th century, under his grandson Kublai Khan who was himself a devout Buddhist, they turned to Buddhism. From the 16th century lamaism penetrated northwards from Tibet and replaced shamanism as a religion.

Shamanism was not confined to Siberia, but spread among all the peoples of the far north. The Eskimos and Indians of Alaska and Canada had witch-doctors, sorcerers and medicine men whose practices were similar to those of the Siberian shamans. Migration from Asia to America was easy as the Bering Straits are only about 50 miles wide and the people on both continents live in similar circumstances and have similar cultures. The

religions of the Finnish-Ugrian peoples of Europe fall into the same category as Siberian shamanism. Several Swedish and Finnish Protestant sects include ecstatic almost trance-like states in their services. Remnants of shamanism have been established in the folklore of the Finns, Estonians and Hungarians.

In other parts of the world too, there are religious practices which are remarkably like shamanism. Many African tribes base their religious rites on self-induced trances and the control of mind over matter practised by Indian yogis has similarities with the shaman's work.

But these links, traces and similarities are not enough; they tell us very little about shamanism in the days when it was the center of religious life among the northern peoples. Unfortunately there are few other sources of information and much valuable evidence has been irretrievably lost. Very little is known about the origins of shamanism. Some scientists believe that certain un-datable cave drawings represent shamans and the objects they used. Since various metals play an important part in the shaman's equipment it has also been suggested that shamanism dates from the Siberian Bronze Age.

The earliest written reference to shamanism is in an Uighur book, the Kutatku *bilik* of 1069 which mentions the word *kam,* shaman. William of Rubronck, the Franciscan papal legate who visited the court of the great Mongol, Khan Moengge in 1254, gave a detailed description of the activities of *chan,* shamans. His report suggests that shamanism was at that time established as the official religion of the Mongol empire. Around the early 1600s, when Russian explorers and conquerors began to roam all over Siberia, these reports increase. There were only scattered references at first, but later complete works were written about the beliefs of the taiga and marsh people.

Early studies were colored by the missionary view which regarded shamanism as the work of the devil. Later, the rationalism of the 18th century saw shamanism as superstition and aberration which could be dispelled by enlightenment and reason. In 1777 shamanism was described as a religion. Writers subsequently compared the shaman faith with the Buddhism of the Lamas and explained the more primitive forms of shamanism as a degeneration. Towards the end of the last century the evolutionist view of shamanism was developed, mainly by the followers of the Russian religious school. Many intellectuals opposed to the Tsarist régime were exiled to Siberia where they studied shamanism as a sociological exercise. They wrote a number of books in which they attempted to explain Siberian shamanism through archaeology and their knowledge of primitive religions.

The 20th century has contributed a number of theories. Followers of the 'Culture Circle' for example, believed that shamanism originated among the primitive hunters of the forest or the nomads of the grassy southern steppes and spread by diffusion. The Swedish writer

According to modern theories shamanism is one of the earlier religions and is peculiar to the environment of nomadic hunters and fishermen.

(Center) Intellectual exiles in Siberia in Tsarist times studied shamanism and wrote books attempting to explain it through archaeology.

Many still believe that only shamans are true healers of the sick and guarantors of good hunting and fishing for the entire community.

Ohlmarks believes that shamanism grew from the rough and precarious life these tribes led under those trying climatic conditions. The great student of religions, Mircea Eliade, believes that the search for techniques conducive to various forms of ecstasy was the decisive factor. And he places the origin of the whole of shamanism to the south. Andreas Lommel turns to ancient history and regards shamanism as the universal symptom of early hunting societies. This is the explanation he puts forward for the pre-historic European cave paintings as well.

Some Soviet researchers believe that shamanism was the oldest religion. Others say that ancestor worship came first. Later scholars call it a tribal religion. Later still, ethnic and ecological considerations prevailed and the various forms of shamanism are emphasized according to place or tribe and to the facts of their historical development. According to contemporary Scandinavian scholars of religion, shamanism is determined by environmental factors. Although it would be easy to conclude that all these views complement each other, even today views of Siberian shamanism have not been fully synthesized.

Shamanism was exposed to many outside influences. Those that came from the south, with lamaism, it was able to hold off for a time. But it was weakened by the coming of Islam and Christianity. It has now submerged almost completely under communism and the changes of the 20th century. Many peoples who had been converted to Islam or Christianity retained elements of shamanism. In the late 19th century shamans among some of the steppe tribes invoked Allah and Judeo-Muslim saints such as Noah, Abraham and David together with their own traditional spirits. Isolated and nomadic peoples especially continued to hold shamanist séances long after the Revolution. Shamanist sacrificial grounds and tombs could be found until quite recently and many chants and rituals are still remembered. The descendants of the most outstanding shamans were sometimes able to profit by their hereditary gifts, talents and acumen by becoming scholars, artists and scientists. Even though traces of shamanism lingered on well into this century, a chapter in the history of human religions came to an end before our eyes, at the same time as a chapter in the history of the peoples of Siberia. The world of healers and intermediaries, establishing contact with supernatural spirits through self-induced ecstasy for some definite purpose, was over. It would be too much to say that our knowledge of shamanism provides a key to the magic practices of the ancient hunters – because it came later than that. Nor can shamanism fully explain the outlook of the tribes who set out from southern Siberia to conquer the world – because shamanism belonged to an earlier and more primitive time. But perhaps it can throw light on life, *mores* and customs as they were between these two important milestones of human history.

47

Khanti and Mansi
Khanti-Mansi National Okrug

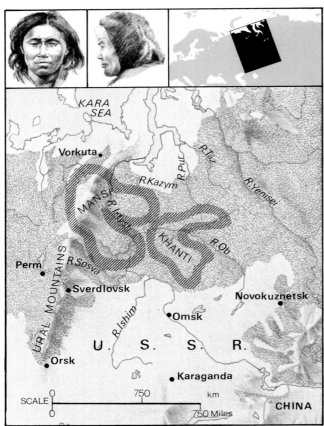

The Khanti and the Mansi live in little groups, separated by enormous distances, on the vast west Siberian plain. Originally they were probably one people who at some time became so separated by habitat and habits that they diverged into two peoples. They are distinguished from each other, but certainly very closely related. The Khanti live on and around the east bank of the Ob' and Irtysh rivers. The Mansi live further west along the Sosva river. Although the languages they speak are distinct they are very similar. They are the more closely associated with each other for being unique in Siberia as Finno-Ugric peoples. More akin to Finns and Hungarians (originally non-European peoples) than they are to their Siberian neighbors they stand out in all Siberia for being linguistically and racially out of place.

The Khanti and the Mansi began their northward and eastward migration from the steppelands of eastern Russia and western Siberia early in the first millennium AD. Their whole way of life had to be adapted to cope with the new conditions which the plainlands offered. They gradually assimilated the older Siberian peoples they encountered on the way, and soon themselves adopted many Siberian ways, discovering for example that the horse, which had once played a central part in their culture, was unsuited to their new home. They made

48

(Top) While out hunting Khanti men build temporary shelters where they can leave the sleds, and lay the traps on skis or on foot.

The Khanti greatly fear the dead and believe they try to capture living souls. Their graves are identical to those of the Nentsi.

their first contacts with Russians in the 10th century. Within 100 years they were regularly trading with merchants from Novgorod and building towns. The intervening years, between those early first contacts and Russian rule later, were dominated by Tatars. The Tatars swept westwards from the Gobi desert in Mongolia and built a vast empire, enveloping the Khanti and the Mansi in the West Siberian Khanate. The Khanti and the Mansi were probably wealthier and more powerful then than ever again. They adopted many Tatar ways and, until the Russian defeat of the Khanate in 1581, they flourished.

The Russians ruled the Siberian tribes through local princelings who collected taxes and administered the law. With the steady increase in numbers of Russians in Siberia the Khanti and the Mansi were driven from the best fishing grounds and land. They were gradually exploited by merchants and traders and demoralized by alcohol and disease. Today there are only 21,000 Khanti and 7,700 Mansi. Yet although numerically small there is among the widely scattered regional groups a huge diversity of language and culture. This can perhaps be put down to the enormous distances that separate them and to the great differences in climate and land.

The vast plain, which rarely rises above 300 feet, is crossed by slow, meandering rivers. There are many lakes and swamps and after the spring thaw, floods cover huge tracts of land. From north to south the climate becomes gradually less severe, and from west to east more extreme. The taiga region, with its sprawling forests and swamps, gives way to the tundra with its sparse vegetation and ground which is frozen rock-hard for much of the year. In winter the temperature can fall to 40°C below. In summer it can rise to 32°C. Such severity and extremes of weather demand a highly specialized way of life. There are three basic activities in these regions around which the lives of the Khanti and Mansi revolve: hunting, fishing and reindeer herding. Nowhere have these people turned to agriculture, although they collect nuts and berries from the forest and tap birch sap to drink. Meat, fish and berries were the sole basis of their diet until very recently when bread and flour became available.

Close to the larger rivers and their tributaries, the Khanti and Mansi's lives focus around fishing. In summer camps they build birch-bark tents on the sandy banks of the streams. They can make huge catches and preserve much of the fish by drying it or smoking it; then they store it to eat in the winter months. They trade any fish that exceed their needs. They eat their fish raw, dried or boiled. They dry the smaller fish and fish heads and then crush them into a kind of fish flour which they add to boiling water to make a fish porridge. They also extract oil from the fish which they either drink or mix with crushed berries and use in soups or pancakes. Even the bladders of the fish are not wasted; they are dried

and made into glue or stretched to become windows for the summer tents. At the onset of winter, just before the rivers freeze, they return to their winter dwellings. These are small settlements with clusters of no more than twelve log huts or semi-underground houses in the forest. From here they fish through the ice in the lakes and streams with rods and lines, fish spears and traps.

Hunting is the major activity for Khanti and Mansi who live far away from the large rivers. In August and September they hunt elk and wild reindeer. Either a single hunter stalks them or they are caught in traps placed at intervals along fences up to fifty miles long, erected across the migration routes. The traps take the form of self-triggering bows. When an animal touches a cord these fire an arrow with such force that it can often pass right through the shoulder blade of an elk. With the first snows in September the Khanti and Mansi start to hunt fur-bearing animals like squirrel and sable in the forest. They hunt them with guns, bows and arrows and traps today, although once they preferred the bow and blunt arrow as it did not damage the fur and was cheaper. This continues until the middle of December when the hunters gather in their winter quarters to trade their furs, pay their taxes and to participate in religious and social ceremonies. Their huts, like the fishermen's, are built of wood with benches around the walls, a fireplace in the center, and ice in the windows, and are

49

The white birch tree is sacred to the Mansi They decorate it with strips of white and red cloth.

The shamanist Khanti believed that men had five souls and women four. Of all animals, only the bear, whom they honored, had four souls too.

Birch trees grow thickly in the taiga. In summer their bark covered the hunting tents and the Khanti and Mansi tapped the trees and drank the sap.

divided into a women's half and a men's half. The hunters return to the forest in the middle of January until the spring thaw in April. Then they move to their summer camp. There they fish and hunt wild fowl. They catch the birds by placing large nets in the birds' flight path between two lakes. They also use decoys and special arrows which whistle like a hawk, making the birds settle and easier to catch. They eat the meat of deer, elk and fowl—both raw and cooked—or preserve it by drying and freezing.

Reindeer herding is not of major importance to the Khanti and Mansi, although they borrowed the techniques from the Nentsi in the 15th century. Conditions were nowhere suitable on the west Siberian Plain, however, for the large-scale herding carried out by the Nentsi. It was the most northerly Khanti, around Obdor, who most nearly imitated the Nentsi way of life. They traded their reindeer products with the more southerly Khanti, but the herds were really only of secondary importance to them. On the Kazym they had herdsmen, but in many places the reindeer were left to themselves until the first snows when they were rounded up, which often took up to two months. The reindeer were important only as transport animals and they were neither killed nor systematically milked. The reindeer would pull the

sledges on seasonal migrations and carry skins and equipment on hunting trips; for shorter journeys skis would be used. Traveling was more difficult in summer because of the swamps and lakes. Then travel was possible only with small birchbark canoes and larger dugouts.

All Khanti and Mansi belong to one of two groups, Mosh or Por, within which marriage is prohibited. The Mosh are thought to be descended from the hare and the goose. The Por are thought to be descended from the bear. These groups hold ceremonies and sacrifices in their respective settlements in autumn and winter. At this time tribes and lineages of Khanti and Mansi also congregate for ceremonies and to settle disputes by ordeals. The general structure of the groups is patrilineal, membership of clans and tribes passing through the male line. They live in extended families which may sometimes include a man and wife, his brothers and families, his parents and his married and unmarried children. As the tribes were so dispersed and lived for so long under Russian rule, there were few wider political institutions, although tribes would unite against a common enemy, splitting again when the danger passed. Today the group structure itself is loosening. Couples of the same group, even the same lineage, will sometimes marry.

The religious life of the Khanti and Mansi was tradi-

The lives of the people along the Ob' revolved around fishing. They erected a stake fence to catch the fish then gathered them in bag-shaped nets.

(Bottom) In winter fishing holes are broken into the ice. A long pole is used, with a net dyed dark brown so as to be invisible in the water.

In the past the Khanti and Mansi never cut their hair; it was braided and adorned with colored ribbons, beads and copper pendants.

tionally rich and intricate. They had many gods and spirits, with whom they communicated through a shaman, who would eat the hallucinogenic fly agaric mushroom to go into a trance. Men were believed to have five souls and women four. Animals were credited with less souls: the bear alone had the same as man. Ceremonies in which the clan and lineage totems were invoked and sacrifices made to the other gods and spirits were held in sacred groves with idols and carvings.

The beliefs and rites centered on the dead are involved with the beliefs about the souls of men. The Khanti and the Mansi believe that one soul lives on in the body until it decomposes. Another soul is believed to go to the underworld, where it remains until it is reincarnated in a new member of the clan. Still other souls are thought to live in clothing and are able to take the form of birds. These souls do not live after the death of their host, who might even kill himself by accidentally shooting one of his souls while hunting. The dead are greatly feared as it is believed that they try to take other souls as companions with them. They are the opposite of the living, invisible to them and doing everything in reverse.

Hunters working in groups trap bears in their dens and kill them with guns and spears and sometimes knives.

Bear festivals are held in honor of the bear after it has

been killed as the bear is thought of as a dead relative whose spirit communicates with other bears and the gods. At the feast the bear is ritually eaten and songs are sung about the life of the bear and his relations with the gods. Then plays are performed about the bear and forest spirits with satirical sketches of the villagers.

The culture of the Khanti and Mansi is rich and vigorous. They have a vast mythology which recounts their heroic past: the wars with the Samoyed, descriptions of their wealth and power and the strength and courage of their heroes. These legends are sung by storytellers to the accompaniment of their traditional stringed instruments.

In recent years many changes have affected their culture: collectivization, schools and clinics and the introduction of agriculture and cattle. But while they rely on the collective centers for equipment and essential services they prefer to live in the still remote regions, in a traditional manner, hunting, fishing and herding reindeer. As the native language and culture have been officially encouraged most Khanti and Mansi are now literate. But although schools for children and access to the outside world provide great incentives for change, the traditional culture is still transmitted to the young and survives as vigorous and adaptable as ever.

51

Nentsi
Northern Siberia

Across the gigantic northern expanses of the world's largest country, the Soviet Union, lives the largest of the 'peoples of the north' as the Soviets term them. The 29,000 Nentsi of the Samoyedic group, the largest of the reindeer people, live much as they have for centuries, herding their reindeer, hunting on land and sea and fishing. Only their primitive technology has been updated. Although they wear some Russian dress, they otherwise remain largely unrussified. They go on wearing their fur boots, deerskin parka and outer fur tunic against the rigorous climate. They live scattered in isolated areas of tundra and forest tundra that stretches from the White Sea on the northern coast of European Russia to the Yenisei river, 1,100 miles to the east, and embraces islands in the Arctic Ocean including the nuclear testing ground of Novaya Zemlya. The majority live in the north of the largest plain on earth, the enormous west Siberian plain, between the two great rivers of west Siberia, the Ob' and the Yenisei, in their three enormous National Okrugs along the Arctic coast.

The reindeer is very much a part of the Nentsi family in the permafrost tundra of the far north: a beast of burden and a source of fur and meat.

Nentsi Northern Siberia

This photo taken in 1884 shows all that is left of the Nentsi women's art. All their skill went into making lavish festive costumes of contrasting furs.

54

Nentsi women's hair is their pride: parted in the middle it is worn in two braids, often lengthened with false braids of colored cloth.

It is a bleak, inhospitable land. Two-thirds lies above the Arctic Circle and all but the southernmost fraction within the permafrost zone. To the north it is open tundra, marsh and lakes, intersected in the west by the Polar Urals which rise to 4,500 feet. Only in the south does the vegetation improve into forest tundra. There are spruce trees west of the Urals and larch to the east. Winter is harsh. The dark days are seemingly endless. Snow can last for 261 days of the year. Temperatures can drop to −54°. Winds blow throughout the year. In winter they blow from the mainland; in summer from the sea. But here fauna abound. There are walrus, seals and white whales, traditionally hunted by the Nentsi; polar foxes and polar bears on the northern coast, reindeer and wolverine in the tundra, salmon and sturgeon in the lakes and rivers and myriads of geese and duck migrating north in summer.

The Nentsi appear to be descended from people who moved from the Sayan Uplands in south Siberia and interbred with the aboriginal settlers who, their folklore relates, lived in dugouts. They were one of the first three Siberian peoples, with the Ostyak and Vogul, to be in touch with the Russians. By the 15th century all three peoples were trading with the Russians settled along the Pechoia. In 1585 the Russians, moving east after the valuable fur, conquered the Siberian Khanate of Khan Kuchum, to which the Nentsi and other tribes of northwest Siberia paid tribute. They annexed the tribes and imposed on them their own fur tribute. Christian missions came only in the early 19th century, when the Nentsi were baptised in families and hundreds of their pagan images burnt at their sacred places.

By this time the Russian traders were exploiting the Nentsi. The Nentsi reacted with organized uprisings against the local tsarist authorities and the Nenets elders. Nevertheless, in the second half of the last century, the Russian impact grew fast. Representatives of large firms followed the individual fur traders into the tundra. Shops were established replacing barter. Fishing enterprises and a river fleet grew up. And the age-old reindeer economy was disrupted.

The Nentsi reindeer breeders who lived in the tundra used herd-dogs and sleds drawn by reindeer. They traveled northwards in spring with their herds and returned south with them in autumn. The ones who lived in the forest grazed their herds in the forest all year round moving to other forest pastures in winter 20 to 60 miles away. Some prosperous reindeer breeders had herds of up to 10,000 head.

The Nentsi also hunted sea-mammals, fished in lakes and rivers with seines 100 yards long, and trapped migrating flocks of ducks and geese in huge net enclosures. They were still using bows and arrows early this century and flintlock muskets up to at least the Revolution.

They lived in conical tents which were in summer made of birch-bark and in winter of reindeer skin. In really

An isolated family is visited by a Russian Orthodox priest. Between his visits the people continue, as they always have, with the old shamanist ways.

(Center) The typical Nentsi sled is made of birch or spruce. The hunter wears skis, fur-covered for longer journeys, and uses traps and self-firing bows.

cold weather they wore a hooded deerskin cape, and fur stockings and fur boots lined with dry grass.

Right up till the Revolution in 1917 the Nentsi retained their clan system in which descent passed through the male line. Each clan possessed its own winter and summer reindeer pastures, its own cemetery and its own sacrificial sites. Although different clans might combine to hunt together relations between the clans could be hostile. Vendettas were often the outcome of inter-clan enmities and rivalries. The Nentsi then might marry up to four wives. Wives were either won by paying a bride-price of up to 200 reindeer or by compulsory work.

Although baptised wholesale by Christian missionaries in the late 19th century the Nentsi retained their pagan beliefs. Indeed they incorporated St Nicholas into their own beliefs, offering him reindeer sacrifices and rubbing his ikon with blood and reindeer fat. They believed that mountains, rivers and other natural features had their 'owner' spirits. They propitiated them or their wooden or stone effigies with sacrifices of food, money, reindeer and so on. The shaman, who would be asked to heal the sick, predict the future and give advice for the hunting would summon the spirits with his tambourine. They worshipped animals, particularly the bear. And each household had its sacred reindeer which was never harnessed or slaughtered.

The Nentsi have been living under Soviet rule for half a century now. Whereas Tsarist policy was basically to leave people like the Nentsi alone, Soviet policy has been to bring the northern peoples thoroughly within the fold. They are encouraged to adapt their economy and lifestyle to Marxist-Leninist principles.

During the collectivization of agriculture the Nentsi like other northern peoples proved troublesome. Reindeer owners responded to the dubious policy of collectivizing their reindeer herds with mass slaughter of their stock. In less than two years the reindeer in the Taymyr area alone were reduced by nearly two-thirds.

Nomadism was regarded as a primitive way of life which held little place in a socialist society. So villages of wooden houses were built for the Nentsi. But it is hard to force nomads to change their age-old ways overnight. Many Nentsi left the houses in which they had been settled completely and returned to live in their tents.

The Nentsi's traditional beliefs, too, came under attack. Shamanism was regarded by the Soviet system as a superstitious practice which must be abolished. The belief survived, however, particularly among the older generation; on the Taymyr peninsula into the late 1940s, any remaining shaman would be shot – if he was caught.

But in education, health and technology the Nentsi are now much better off. Their population rose by over a quarter between 1959 and 1970 to 29,000. And their language is healthy. Only 9 per cent consider Russian their mother tongue. For the forseeable future the Nentsi have a good chance of cultural and ethnic survival.

55

In the Nenets National Area in the Arctic, local women shop in the village store for Russian garments to supplement their home-made fur and leather ones.

Yakut
Yakut ASSR

Unlike the Siberian reindeer herding tribes the Yakut are distinguished as cattle and horse breeders—the origin of their title: 'horse people'.

The Yakut have since the 17th century been subjected to alien influences but have throughout managed to survive as a people. Indeed they not only succeeded in surviving but also in flourishing. Today they maintain their own identity amid a new imposed culture, technology and way of life.

The Yakut call themselves Sakha. They are a three hundred thousand-strong people who live in north-east Siberia mostly in the basin of the great River Lena. They have not always lived here. There is much evidence in their artifacts, economy, social structure, language, religion and art which indicates that the dominant ancestors of the Yakut came from the south, from the Baikal region. Their physical appearance also points to a southern origin. The Yakut have mongoloid features of either the central Asian type – long faces and narrow noses – or the Baikal type – broad faces and flat noses. The Yakut probably reached their present-day region by successive waves of migration. The first wave may have ended in the 10th and 11th centuries, the last around 1500. These immigrants, who included the Buriat (pages 118-123) absorbed some local tribes. And so the Yakut nation of today was born.

Traditionally the Yakut were, and many still are, cattle and horse breeders. Once they were transhumant – moving to northern pastures in summer and returning south for the winter. When the Russians introduced agriculture to Siberia in the 19th century many Yakut became farmers and remain so today. They also hunt and fish for some of their food. And a few Yakut herd reindeer. They learnt this technique from their neighbors, especially the Evenki (pages 110-117). The characteristic Yakut house is a one-storey rectangular cabin which they build of logs. It has an almost flat roof with mud daubed on the outside. The mud serves a special purpose. There is very little precipitation in this region and what there is falls mostly in the form of snow rather than rain. It is very cold and the mud serves as insulation to keep the heat in the houses. The necessity of keeping warm is reflected in the traditional clothes of the Yakut: they are made of hide and fur. The original religion of the Yakut was shamanism, but this, with many other facets of their lives, changed with the Russian arrival in Siberia. In the 18th and 19th centuries most of them were converted to Orthodox Christianity. Conversion was often genuine – only a little shamanism survived into the 20th century.

From the 17th century onwards, when the Russians first came to this part of Siberia, the Yakut have been subjected to many changes. For about three hundred years the name and boundaries of their region were occasionally changed but since 1922 the region has been called the Yakut Autonomous Soviet Socialist Republic, abbreviated to Yakutskaya ASSR or simply Yakutia. Only 4 per cent of all Yakut live elsewhere in the Soviet Union: 9,000 of them in other parts of the Russian SFSR and 3,000 in other parts of the USSR – in the Baltic 57

Yakut fur-trappers live off the moss of the forest as they roam the snows in pursuit of their prey — no less than 22 fur-bearing species.

This is a loaded issue. Difficulties nearly always arise wherever a technologically advanced culture engulfs a relatively unsophisticated one. Usually there are good results, such as a rise in the standard of living, but these tend to be at the expense of traditional ways of life. And the loss of traditions may lead to the loss of national identity. For the Yakut, whose national culture represents a long-evolved response to their harsh environment, its disappearance could have been particularly unfortunate. Either they had to sacrifice their national identity to material improvement or forfeit the chance of material improvement to preserve an impoverished form of their identity. And if they compromised they could just as easily secure the worst rather than the best of both worlds. Those who would like to see the Yakut remain as farmers can be accused of denying them the benefits of industrial civilization while those who would send them down the mines are accused of riding roughshod over national traditions. It is extremely difficult to know exactly what has been happening in Yakutia. Very little on the subject has been published in the Soviet Union and no non-Soviet specialists have been able to visit and study Yakutia. An assessment of how the Yakut are progressing in the new industrial society can only be gained from literature and the few available figures.

The first industry to be established in Yakutia was gold-mining. It was started on the Olekma and the Vitim, tributaries of the Lena in 1846. In 1889 it employed a total of 13,000 people. Only one to five per cent of this labor force were Yakut. And these were mostly employed to manage the horse transport.

Although over the next 25 years the work force doubled, the number of Yakut employed did not increase. At this time most Yakut seem to have been able to resist industrial pressures. However in Soviet times the gold-mining industry continued and Yakut were employed in greater numbers. In 1921 it employed 1,500 Yakut; they were enlisted into the Red Army and from there sent to work in the goldfields. Over the next forty years this number fluctuated considerably. In the second half of the 1920s for example there were no more than 180 Yakut employed while in the early 1930s there were over 1,300 and in 1937, 240. The Yakut seem to have been attracted to this new industry but only stayed on the job for a little while leaving to return to their traditional occupations. Recruiting drives were then held to fill the vacancies.

Meanwhile other branches of the mining industry were established in Yakutia. Some of these seem to have attracted a higher percentage of Yakut. The figures show that the percentage of Yakut employed in the gold-mining industry in 1957 and 1958 was 0·9 and 1·3 respectively while for the same years there were 14·7 and 26·1 in diamond mining, 3·6 and 4·8 in tin-mining, 0·6 and 5·1 in coal-mining and 0·9 and 0·9 in mica-mining. Information on all these industries is extremely scanty but it seems that the Yakut pattern of short term em-

As new settlers swell Yakutia's population Yakut hunters use their ancient skills and knowledge to provide the newcomers with food.

Indiscriminate hunting is banned, and fur-farming as well as trapping is encouraged by the state. Yakutia is now a leading supplier of furs.

(Over page) The setting sun heralds a long cold night as the temperature drops to 65° below but experienced hunters quickly make camp.

61

Yakut Yakut ASSR

To survive in their harsh land the Yakut must know how to adapt. Modern jackets and canvas tents combine with old skills to improve a hunting trip.

(Bottom) As his breath freezes to ice, this Yakut rotates his squirrel-tail hood to keep his nose and mouth warm and dry.

The fur hat with earflaps and fur gloves are essential in Yakutia's climate to prevent frostbite. Even the horses grow extra long thick coats.

On the Lenin collective farm a girl peers out of the triple-glazed window. It is common to ice houses over with snow to retain heat.

Famine used to ravage the Yakut but new foods and farming methods have been introduced and now there is enough food for all.

ployment continued. And it seems clear that up to the early 1960s relatively few Yakut were deeply involved in the mining industry. Furthermore those who were employed did not hold highly 'industrialized' jobs.

Apart from mining, which is the most important industry of Yakutia in terms of the value of the product, there are of course other industries and other forms of employment in which the Yakut are involved – building, transport and communications, agriculture (excluding collective farms), trade, the food industry, culture, science, education, administration and the health services. The number of Yakut working in these jobs rose from 24·1 per cent in 1950 to 26·5 per cent in 1967. When these figures are broken down they reveal that fewer Yakut work in industry (including mining), building, transport, trade and health services but more in education, administration and agriculture.

The sharp rise in agriculture which claims the largest number of Yakut in its work force, as well as the highest proportion, is interesting. It is of course what one would expect given the Yakut's traditions and skills. But there is more to it than this. There has been an actual policy of keeping the Yakut in their traditional occupations. This is evidently justified on economic grounds: the Yakut are the experts at producing food in their own environment. So if more food is required they are likely to be the most skilled at producing it. An economist specializing in these problems wrote 'Maximum use and rational development of the (native) population's traditions, experience and knowledge in particular branches of the economy is the way to secure the most effective, and the most justified, politically and economically, distribution of labor.' And another author writing about the role of the Communist Party among the northern peoples (and therefore presumably knowing something of Party intentions) makes the assumption that the natives will be the food-producers for the desired industrialization program and in this way they will 'hasten the creation of the material and technical basis of communism'.

The other interesting fact is that a high proportion of Yakut not employed in the major producing industries hold cultural and administrative posts. As early as 1724 a Yakut, Trifonov, was appointed military governor. This is very significant as Yakut in these positions can obviously influence policies and thus safeguard their people's interests. The Yakut have always shown an aptitude for things of the mind and are very receptive to education. And they have been quick to pick up Russian skills. Today the Yakut predominate as teachers and office workers.

The intellectual side of Yakut life is flourishing. In spite of the many changes imposed on them there is no sign of an erosion of their national consciousness. The great tradition of poetic writing, which goes back to the 15th century folk epic, *Olonkho*, continues. There are also many Yakut painters and writers. And in 1970 93·6

Reindeer have replaced horses in Yakutia not only as draft animals: at the spring holiday festival Yakut riders race them for fun.

(Bottom) Still popular at festivals is *ohyoxay* where the dancers circle to the left towards the sun – so precious and so rare in Yakutia.

(Bottom) The horse-drawn water cart still makes its rounds through the old quarters of Yakutsk where no plumbing has yet been installed.

per cent of Yakut still regarded Yakut as their first language – the highest proportion of any Soviet northern people. There are newspapers, books, radio and television programs, films and plays all in the Yakut language. When a Yakut child goes to school he is taught in Yakut for the first two years. By the time he leaves school he will be bilingual which will obviously give him an advantage. And many Yakut go on to study at higher levels. There has been an Institute of Language and Culture at Yakutsk since 1935, a branch of the Academy of Science since 1947, and a university since 1956. In the first ten years of its existence the university graduated 3,370 people; 60 per cent of these were Yakut. Today a third of the 15,000 people with higher education in Yakutia are Yakut. And they also represent 28 per cent of the 30,000 people with secondary education. With all these opportunities for education, and given the Yakut natural intellectual aptitudes, it is not surprising to find that Yakuts hold high and powerful administrative posts.

The President of Yakutia is a Yakut woman. A Ya Ovchinnikova. Most of her council of ministers are also Yakut. So are the Rector of the university, the Mayor of Yakutsk and many others. Perhaps more interesting as

an indication of how the Yakut are keeping control of their own affairs is that in 1967 the Secretary of the Communist Party for Yakutia was a Yakut, and so was his deputy. Of course they do not have complete control; there are also many Russian officials but they do not occupy all or even a majority of the powerful positions. The word 'autonomous' in the official title of the Yakut republic often excites scorn in the west. Certainly it does not have the connotation that the Yakut Republic is independent from Moscow, but it does mean that Yakut have a very definite say in their own affairs which they have been quick to take advantage of.

It would seem from the available evidence that the Yakut are fairly contented. It must not be forgotten of course that if they are not it is unlikely that we should hear about it. But there are great financial advantages for the Yakut which could not have arisen had the Russians not in effect been running their country. Since the 1930s the Soviet government has operated a system of pay increments for workers in the northern regions, calculated on a sliding scale depending on remoteness and length of service. Although this system was originally designed to attract immigrant workers to the north and

The villagers of Ehgai have
won many awards for
productivity. They have 5,000
horses famous for their
hardiness and even tempers.

Yakut Yakut ASSR

Permafrost prevents graves being dug in the frozen ground so the dead must be housed in wooden structures like this grave at Irkutsk.

(Bottom) Simeon Pesterev is renowned for his sculptures in ivory and bone. They give him more pleasure than the local television broadcasts.

Snug in his fur garments and ear flaps, with many years of fishing behind him, this Yakut from the Lena River can face anything with a smile.

Modern fishing methods were
introduced to Lena River
fishers in the 1920s, but an
ordinary net can still land
a substantial haul.

to encourage them to remain there in 1960 people already living there became eligible. And in 1968 the rates were increased. Yakut therefore can earn twice as much in their own region than they could for the same job in the south. Nobody learnt quicker than the Yakut the advantage of the maxim 'if you can't beat them, join them'.

In Yakutia at present it seems that a very reasonable balance has been struck between the competing claims of raising the standard of living and preserving national culture. This state of affairs depends on whether industrialization is regarded as good in itself. An economist and planner with a great deal of experience in northern work wrote: 'The industrialization of northern regions, covering areas of settlement of native peoples and reacting beneficially on the development of their economy and culture, creates the preconditions for increasing productivity and improving the organization of labor in the traditional branches of the economy'. Reports on 'ways of drawing the native population into industry' were heard by a conference on population and labor held at Magadan in 1965. But alongside increasing industrialization the Soviet Union also realizes that traditional branches of native economy must be developed, for there

have been cases in the Soviet north where the indigenous people have gone into a non-traditional industry, which has then closed down and left the people high and dry. So for Yakutia the sort of future development which might well prove very successful is the growth of light industry, such as food, clothing or furniture using local materials and, more important, the skills of the Yakut.

The situation in Yakutia is one which most administrators of northern territory in other parts of the world – Canada, Alaska, Greenland, Scandinavia – would regard as satisfactory. In fact they might even find it more satisfactory than what goes on in their own areas. One should add that because the Yakut are certainly more numerous and probably more sophisticated than any northern people living outside the Soviet Union, the Soviet Union has an easier task than other countries. But credit must be given to the Soviet government for the way it has managed the affairs of Yakutia. This seems to show that when there are no pressures to act otherwise, such as doubtful loyalty, closeness to the frontier, ethnic links with foreign countries, the Soviet government is prepared to lean over backwards to put an enlightened nationalities policy into effect – as in the case of Yakutia. 69

Altai
Gorno-Altai Autonomous Oblast

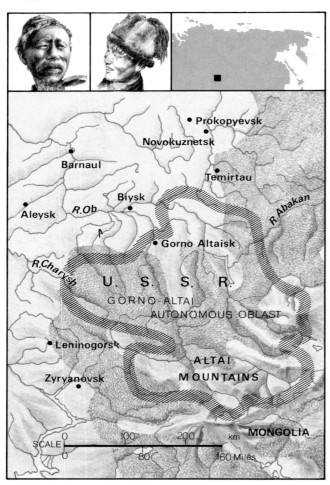

When the Altai became incorporated into Tsarist Russia many of them gradually forewent their nomadic pastoral way of life and became virtually indistinguishable from the surrounding Russian peasants. In the far south of Siberia where they live, a few Altai are hunters, especially those in the northern mountains. A few others work in the towns, but the vast majority are farmers and herders whose way of life has changed little over the past couple of hundred years.

From the Russians, humpbacked or Lithuanian scythes were introduced for harvesting hay. Horses, rather than being used only for transport, might be seen between the shafts, dragging along little two-wheeled carts or loaded with large bags slung across a packsaddle. Or, if the horses belonged to wealthy Altai, they might be pulling hay rakes and mowers. The carter usually rode the horse astride a saddle rather than by the more usual method of driving it from behind.

Today almost any Altai farmer will be wearing a heavy sheepskin overcoat, with a turned down collar, sleeves which are wide at the top and taper into the wrists, the

71

An Altai can become a shaman
after suffering illness and
torment by spirits. The spirit
sings through the magic drum,
symbol of his vocation.

Thick layers of turf make an Altai hut wind- and frost-proof. The new glass window lets in more light than the traditional smokehole in the roof.

whole thing belted with a sash. If he is rich it will be lined with silk. In the past a poor farmer might wear nothing else but his sheepskin unless he also wore a long-sleeved shirt with a diagonal open collar fastened with one button, and a pair of baggy trousers tucked into boots with pointed toes and no heels. Thick felt socks or even grass would keep out the cold. Altai still wear wide-brimmed hats with a ribbon round the crown for adjusting the size. Some wear small round hats with a tassel on top. Women, especially, are loath to cast off their traditional dress of nearly sleeveless overcoats with slits for the arms and tapered at the waist. It was easy to distinguish married women from girls. Married women wore two braids and two earrings whereas girls wore only one of each. The southern Altai wore a pig-tail atop a shaven head but the northern Altai wore their hair long and trimmed in a ring.

The Altai have not always been Russians. The Altai mountains are in that part of southern Siberia bordering Kazakhstan and Mongolia which has always been a cultural crossroads. At different times they have been subject to Turkish, Mongolian and Chinese influences. Turkish influence on the Altai lasted from the 6th to the 8th century. Then in the 12th century they fell under Mongol rule. In the 14th century they came under the domination of western Mongols, the Oriat. When the Chinese defeated the Oriat in the mid-18th century the 12 chieftains appealed to the Russians for protection against China. And so they became Russian subjects.

In those days the Altai were not one tribe but several peoples. In the northern Altai region were the Tubular, Chelkan and Kumandin peoples, while in the southern part, in what is now the Gorno Altai Autonomous Oblast, were the Altai Kizhi, Telengit Telesy and Teleut peoples. Since the Revolution these peoples have considered themselves one people, the Altai. Now they number about 55,000. Only just over half the people in the Altai region are fluent in Russian, and 87 per cent think of Altai, a Turkic language, as their native tongue.

The Altai lived in *yurts*. Some still do. These were wooden buildings of four, six or eight corners, with birchbark covering the roof and the floors. Some of the poorer tribes like the Tubular and the Chelkan built tents of poles set on end and covered with bark. They had neither stoves nor windows but there was a smoke-hole at the top. Other dwellings were round felt *yurts* with dome-shaped roofs. The framework was made of lattice made in several links to which the roof, made of thin sticks was attached, coming together in a ring to let out the smoke. Like Mongolian *yurts* every dwelling had a men's half on the left and a women's half on the right. Opposite the door, which usually faced the river (for Altai settlements were often along the river banks) was the place of honor. People sat on the floor on felt, skins, or birchbark and ate at little tables, round or square with 72 three or four legs.

Wealthy Altai live in four- or eight-cornered wooden *yurts*, with conical roofs covered with birchbark and thick log flooring.

Shamanist Altai consider women unclean and potentially dangerous — property to be bought and sold at marriage and a cheap source of labor.

Their traditionally nomadic way of life was hard and even now their food is not luxurious. As late as 1968 Soviet researchers found that Altai diet – mainly milk, milk products, various roots and porridge – was inferior to the rest of the peoples in the Russian Soviet Federated Socialist Republic (RSFSR). Meat was eaten only on festive occasions or when an animal died of old age. They began to eat better when vegetable growing was introduced.

Altai women had few rights. In such a strongly male-orientated society, their main duty was to look after the household. Among those who practised shamanism women were thought unclean and potentially dangerous. They were regarded as property to be bought and sold at marriage, when they would procreate the male line, and they were, of course, a good source of manual labor. Wealthy women were better off in a material sense, but until after the Revolution they could not hope for an education. Even then a girl had literally to run away from home if she wanted to escape the duties of matronhood. Nowadays such drastic measures are no longer necessary, but still it seems that women must try harder to succeed than men and when they do they are often more successful. Now there are more than 2,000 Altai women members of the Communist Party and somewhat less than half of the deputies to the local Soviets are women.

Shamanist beliefs, similar to those held by peoples throughout Siberia and the Russian far east, were once common among the Altai. A man was called upon to become a shaman after suffering a specific kind of illness during which the spirits tormented him. He might take a familiar spirit or a heavenly bride who sang to his shaman's drum. Every shaman had his own special drum which was also special to the group. He might have several drums. These ornate drums and also the shaman's costumes are being studied today for what they reveal about totemic and other religious beliefs of the Altai. It is virtually impossible to find a shaman today who will perform to an outsider. Because of this reticence it is also difficult to know how many people follow Burkanism, an Altai lamaist movement that condemned many aspects of both shamanism and Christianity.

A shaman's performance, often described in terms of its artistry, might be addressed to either Ul'gen the heavenly spirit or to Erlik, master of the underworld. Women were forbidden to attend the ceremonies to the heavenly spirit, but, according to E M Toshchakova, an Altaian ethnographer, women shamanized within the family group when evil spirits had to be placated. There are still some well recognized shaman clans among the Altai even if it is difficult to learn about them. Pavel Kuckiyak, one of the founders of Soviet Altaian literature, was the third son of a shaman. Since the other two sons had died, and it was thought that evil spirits had taken them, Kuchiyak's parents resorted to a common ruse to ward off the spirits. They named him It'Kulak, Dog's Ear, and placed dog fur in his ears. He survived to tell the tale. Apparently some of the best contemporary Altai folklorists also had relatives who were shamans.

In spite of industrial development in the Gorno-Altai Autonomous Oblast, chiefly mining for gold, mercury, tungsten, molybdenum and marble, most of the Altai live in the countryside. Between 1926 and 1932 there was an increase of four per cent of Altai industrial workers in the Altai region, but they were still only six per cent of the industrial workers living there, the rest being immigrant Russians. Between 1939 and 1959 there was a drop of one per cent of Altai city dwellers, although by 1959 almost twice as many urban Altai were living outside the Gorno-Altai Autonomous Oblast as were living in cities within their native region. In 1970, of the 39,000 city dwellers in the Gorno-Altai Autonomous Oblast 34,000 lived in Gorno-Altaisk, the capital city.

The few Altai who do work in the towns do a variety of jobs. Besides working in the mining industry some of them staff educational, public health and cultural facilities. They help to run the rural economy at an administrative level. Between 1963 and 1969 there were plans made to build schools, pre-schools and public health facilities, houses, and public service facilities. These plans always fell short of their targets. Generally, people in the Altai region are worse housed, less adequately paid and served and less educated than the average among their fellow citizens of the RSFSR.

Tsaatang
Mongolia

Reindeer mean everything to
the Tsaatang. Their name,
given them by their
Mongolian neighbors,
means 'white deer'.

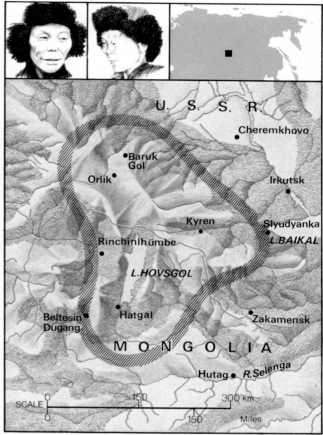

In the far north-western corner of Mongolia, among some of the most remote and inaccessible mountain forests in central Asia live about three hundred Tsaatang. They are the last of the Turkic-speaking tribes of Uryankhai, or 'forest people', to have retained their hard, nomadic way of life wandering around in small family groups, herding their reindeer.

As reindeer herdsmen the Tsaatang are unique among Mongolians. Reindeer provide them with everything to sustain their difficult existence – food, clothing and transport. Reindeer mean everything to the Tsaatang. Even their name Tsaatang – given them by their fellow Mongolians – comes from *tang* 'the people of' *tsaa buga* 'the white deer'. The Tsaatang's almost totally reindeer economy has led to speculation that they may originate from much further north in Siberia. Before the Mongolian Revolution in 1921 the Tsaatang lived in one of the nine banners, or regions, of Uryankhai territory in the Manchu Empire. At the beginning of this century the average Tsaatang family had 29 or 30 reindeer. Only a few rich families might own as many as 200 or 500. The reindeer-breeding Uryankhai were extremely poor; a traveler complained there was no point in sending traders to a region which lacked the most elementary 75

The Tsaatang wigwam is made
of poles covered with cloth
or canvas sheets, or with
the traditional water-softened
birchbark sewn with thread.

comforts. 'All that these people need' he wrote 'is tea, tobacco, two or three sorts of the roughest cloth, gunpowder and a few metal implements. Only the very few people belonging to the more well-to-do class sometimes ask for other things such as flour . . .'

In those pre-revolutionary days they were divided into four main groups based on patrilineal clans. They did not live in clan villages but traveled over the pastures in family groups with their herds. Each family inherited the right to use certain traditional clan pastures. When a young man married he took his wife from a different clan, a share of his father's herd and an allotted series of pastures. With his new wife he started a new herd.

Today about 200 known Tsaatang, 39 families, live among the Darkhad Mongols in the Ulaan-uul, Rinchinlhümbe and Khankh Somons of the Hovsgol Aimak. When these 39 families were studied recently by the Mongolian ethnographer Badamkhatan he found that 13 of them are reindeer herders caring for 1,200 deer, of which 124 belong to the co-operative farms with which they are associated. About 62 families have left and live in the mountain forest by reindeer herding alone.

The Tsaatang live in tepees or wigwams made of poles frequently covered nowadays with cloths, skins and canvas sheets but traditionally with birch bark. The old birch bark cover was warm in winter and kept out the spring rains, but was difficult to transport on the reindeer. Very often it was left behind at one camp and a new cover made at the next one.

A Tsaatang migration is a carefully planned operation. Everything is packed up and prepared by the women the night before. At 7.10 am, according to Badamkhatan, the man of the household goes out to his first deer which is always tied to a post to the south-west of the tepee door. This deer is saddled, bridled and then packed with all the most precious objects of the home. This deer was formerly sacred, consecrated to a spirit, and hung with colored ribbons to show which spirit it belonged to. Women and foreigners were forbidden to ride it. The riding and pack deer are then loaded in order, each with a strictly defined set of goods. Men's deer and goods go in front, women's at the end. The family brew a final pot of tea and, just before setting off, tie the cooking pot on the last reindeer. When they reach the new camping place the men start building the tepee. It takes about an hour to collect all the wood, and the rest of the operation takes about half an hour. The main pole, which has usually been dragged from the old camp, is set up on

The 300 Tsaatang are the last Turkic-speaking tribe of Uryankhai to have retained their traditional nomadic way of life.

(Center) The birchbark tent cover is warm and waterproof, but difficult to transport on the reindeer; it is often left behind and a new one made.

At the beginning of the century it was said of the Tsaatang: All these people need is rough cloth, tea, tobacco, gunpowder and a few metal implements.

the north-west, the windy side, with the other poles leaning together against it in a conical structure. Skins and mats are laid on the earth inside.

The Tsaatang move camp six or eight times every year as they follow their herds. In November they stop for the winter in sheltered hollows in the mountains. It is best if there is a lot of snow; the deer can then reach lichen and grass by pawing through the snow but are prevented from wandering far and tiring themselves. If it freezes hard wolves become a great danger and the deer are tied up round the tepee and let out to graze for a few hours under the careful supervision of the women. Throughout the winter men hunt for meat and furs while the women look after the herds. At this time the deer give barely enough milk to make tea.

Reindeer milk and the milk products made from it are the staple food throughout the summer and autumn. The milk is very nourishing: it has a 14 per cent fat content as opposed to 4.1 per cent in local cow's milk, and contains 2,000 calories per liter while cow's milk has only 766.3. The Tsaatang will rarely slaughter their reindeer for meat.

As spring approaches in April or May the herds become restive and families and animals start moving down to the calving places. It is said that the reindeer will not normally give birth in any other place and sometimes they have to rush, without stopping by night or by day, to get there in time. As soon as the calves are born the women begin milking the mothers four or five times a day while the men travel with the rest of the herd, sometimes up to 12 miles in a day. This is the most difficult time of year. After this they move to summer pastures in July looking for a cool place with no trees. The reindeer are now giving plenty of milk and only go out to pasture in the cool of the early morning or evening to avoid flies. During autumn the Tsaatang move through the forests seeking places rich in lichen and mushrooms to fatten the deer for winter. They finally reach a place near the winter camp where they start cutting grass for hay.

The Tsaatang are virtually the only Siberian people who by their own tradition prepare hay for the winter. The other Uryankhai did this only because they learnt to do so from Russian peasants. The Tsaatang cut the grass not with scythes or reaping hooks but with their ordinary hunting knives. They tie it into sheaves about 20 feet long which they hang from the treetops to dry. In the winter they need only untie the sheaves to obtain sweet-scented green hay.

The Tsaatang were shamanists. Now, according to Badamkhatan, there are only three men in the Ulaan-uul Somon who can reach the ecstatic trance of the shaman. Although Buddhist lamas reached the Uryankhai region they had little influence; like others before and after them, they found it difficult to alter the stubborn tradition of ages.

77

the new Siberians east in their thousands.

Siberian Russians

The Bratsk dam is the world's largest. When completed it will provide power for industries employing over 400,000 people.

the conditions and have to be sent back home. Others, at one time or another, have suffered a form of nervous breakdown peculiar to the Siberian north, especially in the darkness of winter, and it occurs not only among the Russians but among the tribal peoples and others who have to endure prolonged inactivity in the mournful wastelands. Arctic hysteria is basically a mimicry mania. Whatever the victim hears or sees he repeats. He may repeat words he does not understand or he may imitate the noises of animals. If someone stands on his head or turns cartwheels, the hysteric – even if he is very old – will do the same, and continue to do so until he drops from exhaustion.

Naturally the Soviet authorities are as keen to prevent this lamentable neurosis among the new frontiersmen of Siberia as they are to stop their astronauts going mad in the depths of space. Today the Siberian pioneer is kept busy with his work duties and suitably distracted with mobile film shows, amateur concerts, even television. He is fed well, too, and in the remoter parts of Siberia it is possible to eat better and more amply than in any other part of Russia. However, this does not stop the older Siberians from enjoying their time-hallowed custom of chewing garlic as a specific against scurvy. The stench of their highly-spiced breath is one of the

characteristic odors of inhabited Siberia. So, too, is the oily reek of the notorious Siberian spirit, pure 100 per cent alcohol which Siberians use to spike their vodka or down in one on its own. Hard drinking is both a ritual and a recreation in Siberia and much of it goes on to the accompaniment of innumerable toasts. The Siberian alcohol is lethal stuff and the hangover which results from it is a widespread and socially acceptable Siberian phenomenon.

With Siberian spirit in their veins, triple-glazed windows in their houses, insulating walls three feet thick and central heating turned up to maximum, the Siberians keep cosy and cheerful throughout their long winters. But the spring is a season they cannot abide, for the thaw turns the whole of Siberia into a quagmire, and the further north you go the worse it becomes.

When I arrived at the small Russian settlement of Nizhnye Kresty at the mouth of the Kolyma river in June, the snow was just melting and the town looked as though winter had passed through it like a war. Now, in the peacetime of the spring, the inhabitants were emerging from their shelters to survey the battered town and pick among the ruins. During the nine months of winter the people of Nizhnye had jettisoned their waste into the streets outside their houses. But in the thaw the

82

A woman guard has decorated
her railroad crossing hut
with pictures and slogans to
the greater glory of Marxism
and the Soviet workers.

The trans-Siberian Express
has all the romance of the
world's greatest railroads. In
eight days it thunders across
nearly half the world.

(Center) Crisp white linen
covers bunk-beds. In the
daytime they convert into
seats. Selections from Lenin
are provided for travelers.

rubbish of the winter's siege lay exposed in the squelching
mud all over the town; at every turn I came across
discarded bric-à-brac – piles of food cans, a child's
broken toy, a smashed guitar, a sodden mattress, the
carcase of a dog. The wooden houses had been scarred
by prolonged exposure to wind and ice; some leaned at
crazy angles; a few had been ripped apart; the wooden
sidewalks were warped and broken. Worse still the
cesspits had melted and begun to stink abominably.
Only the specialized equipment with which the Russians
fought their winters – the caterpillar-tracked tractors,
the trucks with their enormous balloon tires ringed in
chains, the logs lashed together as huge sledges – passed
through Nizhnye without a struggle.

Summer in Siberia is a sudden, brief excess of sun,
flowers, fruit, fish and mosquitoes. Rooms that only a
few weeks before were warmed by roaring stoves are
now cooled by electric fans in temperatures that may
reach 100°F. At night people drag their beds into
windowless corridors to escape the endless prying light
of a sun that hardly sets. Clouds of voracious little midges
force construction gangs in the taiga to down tools and
to flee.

In this interlude between the end of one winter and
the beginning of the next, the hardy Siberian bares the

83

An engineer boards his trans-
Siberian locomotive at
Khabarovsk. He can look
forward to another 5,800
mile journey back to Moscow.

Siberian Russians

The main road in Bratsk sees few cars but many trucks. Great convoys with chains on their tires ferry supplies during the long winter.

Busy workers stop for a while to read the newspapers and local announcements posted in glass cases in the center of Irkutsk.

more romantic side of his Russian soul. Few people on earth can have such a collective passion for plants and flowers as the Siberians. Every home, office and factory has its pot plants, and flowers stand on the windowsills of every log cabin and apartment block. Every town allocates a substantial part of its budget on planting seeds, bulbs and saplings in any available plot of ground, and takes great care not to destroy all the trees when clearing a new building site. Indeed, some new towns, like Angarsk, an oil center near Irkutsk, or Akademgorodok (Science City), near Novosibirsk, have actually been built inside the forest and designed in such a way that the forest has been incorporated into the lay-out. The squirrels and birds of the taiga continue to inhabit the tall pines, though the pines now stand in city squares.

The Siberians have an intense feeling for nature, for the good earth and its living things. Inside every Siberian, from laborer to technocrat, there is a backwoodsman trying to get out, a forest nomad, hunter, fisherman, naturalist, poet even. For the Siberian has an almost mystical reverence for the taiga, that huge 2,000 mile long tract of conifer forest that covers eastern Siberia in a green pall and provides the world with one of its greatest sources of timber. The taiga is beautiful, silent and mysterious. There are many parts that have never been trodden by man. Among those limitless cedars and evergreens a man can enjoy for a while a sense of freedom and self-determination, and in the Soviet Union especially this is a great privilege. To understand the Siberian's attitude to the taiga is to understand the Siberian. It explains why the worst insult a Siberian can give a man is to call him an ink soul, for ink soul means a bureaucrat, especially one from the big cities on the other side of the Urals, a being who is the very antithesis of everything the taiga stands for.

The taiga is a true wilderness and no place for tyros. There are many dangers – swamps, wolves and bears, poisonous insects, forest fires, hunger and exhaustion. Old taiga hands, called *taiozhniki*, never set off without a basic outfit which includes an axe, a knife, a saw, a kettle, a frying pan, a rifle and a means of making fire. They wear fur socks in winter and a face veil in summer, and they know how to live off the land and which direction to go without using a compass. Above all they can read the forest signs to predict the weather, for the weather is the key to their survival. A clear night without dew means rain the next day; rings round the sun mean snow in twelve hours; the crackling of dry wood means frost; frogs croaking in the daytime means rain; fish jumping for insects means stormy weather; swallows flying high means fine weather. If smoke from a campfire goes straight up, it means frost; if it billows, it means a storm; if it hangs close to the ground, it means a thaw.

Over the course of 300 years the Russian settlers have learnt the survival techniques and forest lore of the aboriginal tribes of Siberia in much the same way that the Portuguese colonists in Brazil learnt from the Indian tribes of the interior. This Siberian folk tradition is especially rich in medical lore and a great many herbal remedies have been acquired from the old shamans. A few years ago these were regarded as pure mumbo-jumbo. Today they are the basis of a new science called ethno-botany and every year a number of medical expeditions set out to investigate the folk healers of the remotest communities. Some of the recipes are clearly useless; others seem to effect some magical cure. Here are a few of them:

Onions in vodka, or birch buds in vodka, for intestinal parasites.

An infusion of pine needles for scurvy and vitamin deficiency.

Suppositories of grated raw potato for haemorrhoids.

Dry blackberry leaves boiled in hot tea for stomach-ache.

Cobwebs to stop external bleeding.

Burying the patient up to his neck in manure for rheumatism.

There are hundreds of such remedies in Siberian lore, most of them dependent on an intimate knowledge of the

For the young workers who
have settled in the new towns
they have helped to build,
marriages are frequent
occasions for a celebration.

85

A young factory worker, dead
from poisoning, is buried at
her kolkhoz (collective). A
foreman gives the speech, and
there is a red star on her grave.

most obscure plants. But the few people who still use them are a dying generation. The new Siberians regard them as comical anachronisms. After all, there is a modern medical service widely available to all.

Among these new Siberians there are prospectors and scientists on scientific expeditions. They huddle around lonely camp fires one can see from the air at dusk. These dedicated young men and women, hundreds of miles from the nearest settlement, are the so-called possessed ones – volunteers who choose to lead a lonely and dangerous life wandering all over the wilds looking for gold and diamonds, copper, oil, iron and other minerals.

Most of the prodigious discoveries that have been made in Siberia in the last ten to fifteen years have been made by these people. Often they are dropped by parachute and for months on end they must make their way through virgin country on foot. Many of them have disappeared without trace. Many of them, because of the shortage of young men after the war, are women. It was a woman, Larisca Popougaeva, who was dropped by parachute into the outback of Yakutia and discovered at Mirny one of the biggest diamond fields in the world. Women play a very conspicuous part in the development of Siberia. They tend to be more stable and dependable – and more sober – than the men and they share the hard jobs like welding, concrete mixing and operating cranes equally with men, and enjoy the same pay and privileges.

What is it that drives these people from the more comfortable cities of western Russia to volunteer for a hard and often rough and crude life in Siberia? In part it is in response to a patriotic call to duty. In part it is a desire to lead a more exciting and fulfilling life, to escape from the boredom and regimentation of so much of Soviet society. In part, too, it is the lure of the 'long rouble', the high pay. It is possible to earn big money in Siberia by ordinary Russian standards. A long-distance lorry driver in eastern Siberia can earn as much as a doctor in Moscow, and a Leningrad engineer on a short-term contract in Yakutsk can earn five times what he would earn at home. Pay increases with latitude and in the Arctic regions it can be as much as 100-200 per cent above the normal rate. It also increases with length of service, ten per cent being added for every one or two years served.

If to the far north hardship bonus you add the same conditions that all Soviet workers enjoy – low rent, free medicine, free education, negligible income tax, almost free public services, practically free holidays, an early pensioned retirement and the fact that most wives also work and therefore contribute to the family income – then it becomes clear that service in Siberia can be a lucrative and attractive business.

When the money incentive was first introduced during the Kruschev era it was not considered a particularly Soviet way of going about things. But with the dissolution of the slave labor camps after Stalin's death a huge influx of workers and technicians was urgently needed to develop the immense resources of Siberia.

These resources really are prodigious. The Russians now have a geological map of the entire Siberian region down to 10,000 feet below the ground and new deposits are discovered with monotonous regularity. Siberia has 80 per cent of the Soviet Union's coal, a quarter of the world's timber, colossal reserves of oil and natural gas, and an abundance of gold and diamonds. It has more iron ore, manganese, tungsten, lead, nickel, cobalt, asbestos and bauxite than any other country. Its hydro-electric potential is limitless – the Lena river alone, with its tributaries, is expected to produce twice as much electricity as Britain's present output from *all* sources.

Siberia is Russia's new world and is progressively becoming the economic heart of the Soviet Union. The Siberians are enormously proud of their country and have a breathtaking vision of its future. They envisage harnessing surplus electricity and underground thermal springs to centrally heat the northern regions, melting the permafrost that covers so much of the country, and enclosing the towns in air-conditioned plastic domes illuminated by artificial sunlight during the long Arctic nights. They envisage reversing the direction of some of Siberia's rivers and irrigating the southern steppes so that they can grow enough food to feed an eventual Siberian population of 250 million. They see Siberia as a crucial factor in future human life on this planet. At Akademgorodok (Science City) the best brains co-ordinate all the scientific research in Siberia and devise a program which will transform Siberia into one of the richest and most productive regions in the world.

In the last 15 years several hundred new towns and settlements have been built, along with a number of industrial complexes and a new trans-Siberian railway line. These new towns are not totally raw frontier towns, they have not evolved slowly by chance; they are planned beforehand and constructed as self-contained packages, complete with squares and parks, theaters, museums, scientific institutes, schools, hospitals, stadiums and ubiquitous little statues of Lenin. In terms of fecundity and virility they are breaking Soviet records. During the construction of the new town of Angarsk (population now over 200,000) 35,000 babies were born to the work teams; at Bratsk dam, where the average age of the workers was under 25, there were 300 births every month.

Today Siberia has all the frenetic excitement and cock-a-hoop pride and ambition that must have marked America's expanding frontiers a century ago. There, in the new communities growing up in the heart of the forest, the antique values of the pioneer, the old hardiness, self-reliance and independent spirit of the *Sibiriak* are perhaps taking over from the acquired or imposed *mores* of Moscow. Siberia is the country of the future they will never stop telling you there. To which others reply 'The future is already here'.

Babies are well cared for in a collective's day nursery while their mothers work to provide food for Siberia's rapidly growing population.

The new Siberians

Siberia was acquired by Russia during the 16th and 17th centuries. The largely peaceful process began in 1581 when the Cossack leader, Yermak Timofeevich, was sent by the Stroganov family who owned factories and mines in the Urals to retaliate against and discourage raids by Siberian tribes. Yermak set out with 840 men and, with the advantage of firearms, defeated the far larger forces of Tatars. He took the Tatar khanate of Sibir in October 1582. Russian towns were founded, initially as forts and outposts with only a little rudimentary agriculture in the immediate vicinity. Rapid expansion followed. The Pacific was reached in 1639.

The ghost town of Mangazeya was an interesting example of this process of Russian colonization. Mangazeya was the first Russian town in the Arctic Circle, founded at the turn of the 16th and 17th centuries on the River Taz. Known throughout the world as a source of sable-skins, it was the yearly gathering place of Scandinavian, English, Dutch and Danish merchants. Here local traders bought furs and skins from hunters for next to nothing; trade flourished and the town grew. The town's growth and the uncontrolled incursions of foreigners who avoided customs duty alarmed the Tsar

Party ritual is strictly observed in Siberia. These 'Young Pioneers' salute and cheer on the 'Day of the Rally of the Flags'.

In a school laboratory at the University of Irkutsk, Lenin looks down on the future scientists of his once backward country.

Siberian Russians

The local party secretary is the strong man of each kolkhoz. From behind his desk he decides and dictates; the party will always back him.

of fortunes. Many were forcibly transported to the Siberian tundra and taiga. Under the Tsars many including criminals, heretics against the Orthodox church and adherents of various illegal sects were exiled or imprisoned in Siberia. Political and literary protestors were exiled as well. These included Radishchev, Novikov, Dostoëvsky, and Chernyshevsky, the Decembrist rebels of 1825 and participants in the Polish uprisings of 1830-1 and 1863. Later Lenin, Stalin, Trotsky and most of the Bolshevik establishment had terms of exile in Siberia. Stalin, in fact, was there three times.

In 1860 Dostoëvsky, after four years as a convict in Omsk and four more in a penal battalion in Semipalatinsk, gave this account of life in Siberia in his *Notes from the House of the Dead*:

'In Siberia generally life in the civil service is very cosy in spite of the cold. The people here are simple, non-liberal. Their ways are old, unshakeable, and sanctified by centuries. The officials, who in all fairness play the role of a Siberian nobility, are either indigenous, confirmed Siberians or men who have come from Russia, mostly from Petersburg or Moscow, lured here by disproportionate rates of salary, double allowances and attractive prospects for the future. Those of them who know how to solve the riddle of life almost always stay in Siberia and happily put down roots. Subsequently, they bear abundant and rich fruit. But the others, flippant people who are not able to solve the riddle of life, soon tire of Siberia and ask themselves miserably why they came here. They impatiently serve out their term of duty, three years, and on its termination immediately fuss about their transfer and return home where they came from, reviling Siberia and mocking it. They are wrong: not only from the point of view of work, but also from many other points of view, it is possible to live in bliss in Siberia. The climate is magnificent; there are many remarkably rich and hospitable merchants, many extremely well-to-do non-Russians. The girls blossom like roses and are moral to the ultimate extreme. Wild game flies along the streets and barges into the hunter of its own accord. An impossible amount of champagne is drunk. The caviare is amazing. The reapers in some places take only 7 per cent of the harvest for their wages. All in all it is a blessed land. All that is needed is to know how to exploit it.'

The building of the trans-Siberian railway in the 1890s and government encouragement to peasants to settle in Siberia boosted the population and began the exploitation of Siberia's natural resources, continued by Stalin's industrial policies and deportations of the 1930s and '40s. As many as 20 million were estimated to have been exiled and imprisoned by Stalin, although not all were sent to Siberia. No-one escaped from Siberia in those years, and not many survived. Only later in the 1950s was such a vast migration again to cross the Russian steppe to Siberia. But this time it was in search of adventure and fortune.

and his boyars in Moscow, who feared the foreigners might even colonize the hard-won Siberian territory. The sea-route to Mangazeya was forbidden on pain of death. The fur-traders and others began to leave, mostly for Turukhansk further east. Then, in 1642, Mangazeya was totally destroyed by fire. Today its site is overgrown by tundra.

The men and women who first settled these far-flung, isolated, freezing outposts of the Russian empire were bold, rugged and often desperate. There was no missionary zeal to explain their enterprise. Indeed, as a tribute of furs was levied on non-Christians, the church was instructed to baptise as few as possible of the native tribespeople. The Russian 'overlanders' who crossed the Urals (then known simply as The Stone) included free Cossacks, fur traders and people who had been sent to the Urals and beyond to serve Moscow and who deserted to join other refugees in the new lands. They followed the rivers and tributaries – and they settled.

The settlement of Siberia was only partly spontaneous, however; people were not always drawn by the promise

The harsh and monotonous climate makes Siberians inordinately fond of flowers. In their absence, printed and embroidered ones will do.

(Bottom) Siberians heartily enjoy their drinks. The women of remote Abrashino queue all morning for the twice weekly beer delivery.

A sunny day in the village of Baikal on the lake. The thawing snow will soon turn the unpaved roads into long muddy sewers.

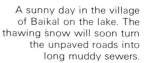

The Siberian's character today is more a product of his environment than a legacy of his predecessors or Siberia's history. To survive demands physical toughness but also doggedness. A Siberian never accepts defeat. In a blizzard he knows that to stop moving means to freeze to death. And if the official channels are cumbersome he will find some rough and ready unofficial solution. Siberia is, after all, a long way from Moscow and it takes a long time for anyone in Moscow to do anything about it. There is a tendency to improvise, to bend officialdom. Railwaymen, on a day off, go berry-picking in the forest and then wait by the line for a friend to give them a lift. The thundering double-headed diesel with 60 bogie oil-tankers screeches to a walking pace to allow one man with a rucksack full of whortleberries to get home an hour sooner. A group of nurses go mushroom picking in the woods one Sunday in the hospital's padded van. Or, before the new year, the night mail train stops in the forest for half-an-hour while the postmen set to with axes, and half the town turns out at two in the 89

Siberian Russians

Siberian boys, if not at school, must work however young. These cattle-herders seem to enjoy the sun as the horses enjoy the pasture.

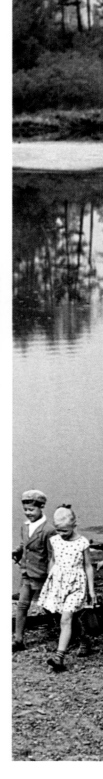

morning to buy cut-price Christmas trees.

After waiting an hour for a bus that never comes, no-one seems to mind paying a passing lorry driver half a rouble for a ride that should cost a tenth of that price. The peasants who offer their vegetables for sale in the courtyard of a block of flats 40 minutes away from the market are occasionally fined five roubles and moved on by the police, but they keep coming back. One day, one imagines, the authorities will have to build them proper stalls. A motor-boat on the Ob' river, near a jet fighter factory at Novosibirsk, is made of supersonic shaped drop-tanks. During a foot-and-mouth epidemic which prevented all movement of animals and people from certain villages a Siberian woman was proud of having trudged 15 miles through the forest with her baby to skirt the pickets and rejoin her husband; she couldn't have cared less about the epidemic. If this approach to life is characteristic of the Soviet Union in general, in Siberia it is quite unashamed.

And then also some old habits and customs linger on in Siberia. If, for some unexplained reason, a trans-Siberian train stops in deep country, miles from anywhere, people get out to pick wild flowers after a little while. The engine-driver sounds the whistle loud and long to recall his straying flock when he is ready to proceed. The last shadow of another old custom, apt to make younger people smile patronizingly, is enacted when someone is leaving on a journey. It is customary, when the traveler's luggage is packed and all is ready, for everybody to sit down with him in silence for a few minutes. This little ceremony dates from the days when going on a long journey was dangerous and it could be years before the traveler returned – indeed if he did return. During the silence the traveler was supposed to ask forgiveness of everybody for any wrong he might have done them. Today the person departing is not expected to say anything. But the silence is effective. Even now, when the 2,500 mile train journey to Moscow takes only two and a half days, who really knows whether all will meet again?

Siberian city life is not significantly different from life in any Soviet provincial town. Housing is adequate and a young couple can look forward to acquiring a flat by waiting in the housing queue or by joining a co-operative of their colleagues from the factory or the institute to build their own block of flats with a 50 per cent interest-free loan from the state.

The flats are very small: one room for single people

90

Siberians like to make the most of the brief warm spells. A nature walk beside the lake is a rare escape from the schoolroom.

Being a sun-worshipper can be very frustrating in Bratsk; hot weather means stifling nights and mosquitoes as well as pleasant country outings.

Women play an important part in Siberian history and its economy. They have equal pay and privilege and do the same jobs as men.

This lady tram driver is very proud of her smart uniform and shiny vehicle. Siberian women also drive cranes and locomotives.

(Bottom) The high wages encourage workers to move east; this factory worker earns twice as much as she would in Moscow.

and two rooms for a family. Every flat has a small kitchen and a tiny bathroom and lavatory, which usually has no windows. There is a small balcony, useful for drying, washing and storing food in the winter, and a little hall, essential for holding all the paraphernalia of bulky outdoor winter clothes and boots. Because the blocks are often inhabited several years before the rough ground between them is tidied up, it is customary in all seasons for everyone to change their shoes just inside the front door. There are no letter-box slits on the doors. Every family has its own locked letter-box at the bottom of its particular staircase. There is no room for dustbins on the tiny landings outside the three or four flats on every floor, nor, of course, inside the flats. Twice a day women come round with a lorry and people carry their own rubbish-containers down to them.

Central heating is universal, piped from a district boiler house and switched on in the autumn and off in the spring. That way it comes cheap, and to a Siberian an individual boiler would seem uneconomic. Electricity, water and gas are also supplied very cheaply. But in summer hot or cold water may suddenly be cut off for days at a time without warning. Lifts are compulsory in buildings of over five storeys, but their maintenance comes low on the list of municipal priorities. When the lifts stop there is no alternative but to start climbing the stairs. In Novosibirsk, Siberia's largest city with a population of over a million, the public transport system also seems to come low in the priorities, and is inadequate and undermanned. To squeeze even more passengers up the bus towards the exit doors at the front and allow those still struggling at the back to clamber in, a driver normally accelerates and then brakes hard, sending a human surge forwards. No-one gets seriously hurt because the crush makes it impossible to fall.

The shops are not well supplied. There are seasonal food shortages – perhaps eggs one month and milk the next. Then, perhaps as the result of a local outbreak of foot-and-mouth disease, meat is short. Or after fires in the grain elevators (which could not be put out because

Female ditch-diggers are a
common sight in Bratsk. They
are indispensable on the
construction sites of this
rapidly expanding town.

the fire-brigade did not know the water had been cut off in that district) bread becomes scarce. Even kettles were unobtainable in Novosibirsk for five years – curious, in this city of aero-engineers, turbine fitters and nuclear technicians. When asked why no-one writes to the papers to complain, it was explained that then there would be nothing but kettles in the shops for the next five years. When people go shopping they consequently take the attitude that if there is a queue, join it, whether or not they know what they are queueing for – it just might be that long-unobtainable and cherished glass dish. Although there are, for many Siberians, more urgent things to do than indulge individual fancies, Moscow and Leningrad with their relatively high standards of living tend to be scorned as decadent. Factory workers in Siberia do nevertheless earn high wages. And lack of consumer goods to absorb these high earnings releases a great deal of money for spending. Much of their high earnings is spent on alcohol. Perhaps the potential supply of private cars will remedy the situation – as high taxation on alcohol failed to do. The first Russian-built Fiats (the Soviet version of the people's car) have recently reached Novosibirsk. There are fortunately often

wholesome alternatives to drinking. In Novosibirsk there are cinemas, a two-thousand-seat opera house and many sports grounds. Fishing is free, but the hydro-electric dam has damaged fish life, so there is little to be caught. Sterlet (small sturgeon) are now virtually extinct – not that the drillers of holes through the ice or the summer anglers seem aware of it.

While for many urban Siberians there is a considerable pride with the way things have turned out, their romantic dream must be somewhat tarnished. Sometimes a sad, resigned respectability descends. The famous science town of Akademgorodok, a suburb of Novosibirsk 25 miles to the south, was founded in 1957. Sixteen institutes and a computer center employ about 25,000 scientists and engineers. It was originally intended that the scientific discoveries should be developed for practical use in Siberia. The results have not yet been as exciting as the mainly young and enthusiastic scientists had hoped. They are now ten years older and they have settled into a solid routine. The famous café, *The Sign of the Integral,* which was once as lively as a night-club, is now *Canteen No 36,* the exhibitions of Soviet artists of the 1920s and 1930s (whose work was suppressed by Stalin and never seen 93 publicly) have been stopped since the organizer was arrested for faking ikons and selling them to western visitors.

The people who live in the blocks of flats which replaced the picturesque wooden or half-wooden houses of the traditional village type in Novosibirsk miss their own back gardens. Their apartment balconies support amazing growths in summer, but if they really want to grow their own fruit and vegetables they have to rent an allotment outside the city, probably miles away and not on a city bus route. Better still some can obtain a *dacha,* or summer cottage. Plots of land for *dachas* are allocated to organizations and industrial concerns and the individuals selected are probably the most energetic, ambitious or influential. Many of the materials will have fallen off the back of state-owned lorries. But the state seems eager to support these *dacha* settlements.

The ground which surrounds every *dacha* is turned into a garden and the family may be picking the first currants or raspberries long before the house is finished. The manic activity at *dacha* sites belies any notion that they are for relaxation. Timber is provided and plans may be available, but the results are the product of shameless individualism. They vary from the practical simplicity of a surplus railway carriage brought in through the mud by lorry, or a log house from the town which is dismantled with each log numbered and then reassembled on site, to romantic multi-storey and elaborately decorated follies. The Russian love for his traditional building is allowed full expression. The hammers and saws start at daybreak and no design is ever complete: the porch is always being put round the other side, a room is being added where the front door was, or the privy is on the move to the other end of the garden. Every weekend the *dachnik* is slave to his folly.

Using the *dacha* to stay in will at first be more a matter of camping out and has a great appeal for city-dwellers with a nostalgic feeling of adventure and pioneering. Then gradually a room will be finished, a veranda glassed in, windows mosquito-proofed (a necessary amenity), a starling's nest-box fixed to the nearest tree – starlings are almost the only birds Russians can recognize and are considered the herald of spring – and finally, after some years, instead of all water having to be laboriously carried uphill from an artesian well, piped water may be arranged. Life is now comfortable and civilized, but the first flush of adventure has fled.

I remember going out to one unfinished *dacha* for a

Russian Orthodox churches receive not the slightest support from the state, but are lovingly kept by the old believers.

No new churches are built in Siberia. Many old ones are closed. Others have been converted into museums or film studios.

The sandy shores of Lake Baikal are a favorite summer picnic spot. Melons and tomatoes are enjoyed while they last.

day in late spring, taking picnic food and having to wade with it across a river. It was long before the ferry had started working or the rickety wooden footbridge had been put up for the coming summer. Soup was heated on a make-shift stove in a corner of the garden, but it was a surprise to discover our drink was iced champagne (Novosibirsk brand). This was explained by the ice-cellar dug into the permafrost. Its heavy wooden cover was fastened with a padlock. Steps led down into a kind of larder, where provisions such as butter and champagne lay on shelves of ice. This icy hole in the ground provided a natural refrigerator throughout the three months of summer. During these months many families may migrate to the *dachas* for several weeks. A *dacha* is supremely elastic in the number of people it will hold.

There are still villages and peasants in Siberia. At the southern end of Lake Baikal, 1,000 miles east of Novosibirsk, a train makes a daily three and a half hour journey down the old single track line from Stantsia Baikal on the south bank of the Angara river as it leaves Baikal. Lights from the villages on the far shore of the lake are visible as the train sets off an hour before dawn. It stops about forty times at settlements which sometimes consist of only two or three wooden cottages huddled at the bottom of a steep gulley. The halt may be little more than a ravine with a stream tumbling down to the lake, a fishing boat on a shingle beach, a hayrick, stacks of firewood and steep cliffs on each side into which the line tunnels.

The train fills up with villagers as it approaches the timber port of Kultuk and curves round the south-western end of the lake to Slyudyanka, a railway town where the new trans-Siberian main line comes down from the hills, double-tracked and electrified. The rumble and hooting of shunting trains never ceases. In this town the market has fresh produce but the shops are inconsistent – no milk and not even vodka, only drinking spirit, but plenty of sausage. From Slyudyanka another local train continues round up the south-eastern shore of the lake, passing the huge new cellulose plant at Baikalsk, the center of an environment controversy in the Soviet press. The train loses most of its younger passengers here. The others are returning to the older villages up the lake side. They urge you to stop at Vydrino, which turns out to be a dusty village with a factory belching pitch-black smoke out of a tall stove-pipe, and they cannot understand why you should not want to visit this triumph of industry and why you should buy another ticket from the conductor and then get out at a halt which has no name except the indicator of its distance from Moscow, '5392 kilometers', where there is nothing except a sandy beach, hundreds of sun-bleached trees washed up by autumn storms and a view across the clear waters of the lake to the blue mountains you edged along that morning. There is no-one else in sight until a suspicious fisherman arrives. He is worried in case you are a fishery inspector and, once satisfied, sets

Summer evening concerts need no artificial lights here: the Siberian sun makes up for its long winter absence by not setting at all.

Siberian Russians

Siberia's early pioneers lived
in tents and wooden huts.
Now, every year, the homes
become warmer
and better equipped.

In a modern shop in Bratsk there is no lack of hygiene. The cleanliness makes it all the more obvious that there is little there to buy.

Just off his plane on Bratsk airstrip, this old man is dressed in his best clothes: it is a classic Russian costume complete with bowler hat.

out in his boat to a point about 400 yards from shore to fish with a line, which is legal, and probably also with a net, which is not. There is a ban on fishing for the unique Baikal *omul'* which innumerable poachers circumvent. Generally, round Lake Baikal, the village people are much more attentive and ready to smile than in the industrial towns. It is a region with character and a uniquely Siberian beauty.

Tenga in the Altay mountains is a very self-sufficient village dedicated to sheep-farming. It is a long way from the fleshpots and in winter is snowed in. The villagers grow much of their produce on their private plots, pick and preserve berries – various currants from the taiga south of the village, wild gooseberries from the rocky slopes to the north. Some keep bees and most have chickens and the permitted cow. The cows are looked after during the day by a village cowherd who is paid a rouble a month for each cow and may well be the best-paid inhabitant.

In summer, at Tenga, the sheep are pastured over the other side of the mountains, protected from wolves and bears by armed shepherds. In winter they are kept in pens and fed on hay scythed in the summer from the valley and the lower slopes. The houses are clean, and the water from the river which drains the taiga is pure and very cold even in August. A particular hazard in May, as in much of Siberia, comes from encephalitis ticks, insects that drop from birch trees and hide in the inconspicuous parts of the human body, like the armpits. People may not know they have been bitten and posters exhort husband and wife to inspect each other minutely. Some villagers are infected each year; the disease makes them slow and mild in temperament and it can prove fatal. The ticks appear to have spread across Siberia after the war and rumors blame the Japanese.

In the short summer firewood has to be chopped for the big brick stoves set in the middle of the log houses. Here the women cook bread, and here also the grand-fathers sleep. There may be ikons on the wall above the

bed but there is no church in the village of Tenga and no priest. A seven-year school has been replaced by the standard Soviet ten-year school. Twice a week in the summer, a traveling cinema arrives and a shop now sells a variety of consumer goods. In years past the only thing required and consumed in phenomenal quantities was vodka. Even now, in the afternoons, figures can sometimes be seen sleeping it off in the roadway. But they are charitably dragged out of the sun by passers-by as the shadows move round.

At the southern end of the 100 mile long lake formed by damming the Ob' upstream from Novosibirsk, the village of Abrashino is a sleepy backwater in the pine-woods, a belt of which stretches up to Berdsk. Communication with the outside world is by river – either by the daily ferry and a bus over to Kirza or by diesel river-steamer to Novosibirsk or Barnaul. The active men and women of the village, if they have not moved to the town, often camp on the logging site, for forestry is the major industry here. Most of the remaining population are very old or very young. One 86-year old woman still has perfect hearing and twice daily humps two buckets of water on a yoke from the well. Sparrows perch on the

97

(Over page) Novosibirsk, founded in 1893, is the largest city of Siberia, an industrial center and a distribution center for grain, meat and timber.

Siberian Russians

buckets of drinking water and the air is filled with flies. The old folk are Baptists; they have no books except a bible and leave the speaker of the piped radio permanently unplugged. The village shop sells tinned food and hardware and clothing. On Saturday the arrival of beer in a huge barrel produces a two-hour queue which behaves itself unusually well.

To lessen the differences in living standards between townspeople and villagers is a major concern for Siberia's administration. When the peasants were backward and led relatively simple self-supporting lives, the most important tasks were to provide education, electricity and agricultural machinery. Now that these, together with radio if not television, films and improved communications with the towns are available, the ways of villagers draw closer to those of factory workers and townspeople. The passive attitude of the past is giving way, in some villages at least, to the energetic initiative and assertiveness of the industrial age; the peasant is no longer the victim of his environment, he creates and controls it. And he drives his noisy machine across the steppe with a new awareness of his actions.

Today the Siberian villager demands a standard of

100

Since prefabrication plants are limited to two or three types of building most new Siberian towns are deprived of individuality.

(Top) Cement pillars are forced into the permafrost after the ice has been melted with steam: this is the only way to build in Yakutsk.

Siberians often supplement their winter diet by fishing in the lakes and rivers. City dwellers enjoy fishing in their leisure time.

As Lake Baikal freezes over solidly enough for heavy sleds to travel over, the fisherman must first break a hole through the thick ice.

Siberian Russians

One of the Soviet government's incentives to attract people to Siberia was the private plot given to peasants on the collective farms.

For Siberians living on
sea shores swimming is a
religion. Bathing suits and
flippers are casually worn
at 35°C below zero.

living equal to that of industrial workers. He may have bought a motor-bike and not be able to get petrol or spares easily. He may have technical qualifications as a mechanic or electrician yet find that he has to spend a lot of his time working in the fields with other members of the collective farm. So he moves to the town, where he has a greater range of opportunities in work, further education, entertainment, social life and consumer goods. To meet these growing demands in far-flung villages requires action. Half measures like mobile shops only seem to whet the villagers' appetites.

These are among the major problems facing Siberia today. They are not really anything to do with Siberia's place in the Russian conscience, though her reputation is hardly enviable. Inevitably the salt-mines are ingrained in everyone's response to the very word Siberia. But that response also includes a recognition of Siberia's potential benefits. Russians have an ambivalent attitude. They associate it with the camps, mosquito-ridden swamps and freezing desolation on the one hand and, on the other, boast of Siberia as a land flowing with vodka and diamonds, a country of forest swaying in the fragrant breeze, of pristine, fish-filled rivers and lakes, of horizon after horizon of promise and of men who are men. Siberia certainly has a past, a history of men, misery and mournful wastes. But above all, Siberia has a future that already gives a glimpse of what tomorrow will be like.

Many of Siberia's native
tribesmen still follow their
traditional occupations of
hunting and trapping. The furs
are now brought to factories.

Udege Khabarovskii Kray and Maritime Kray

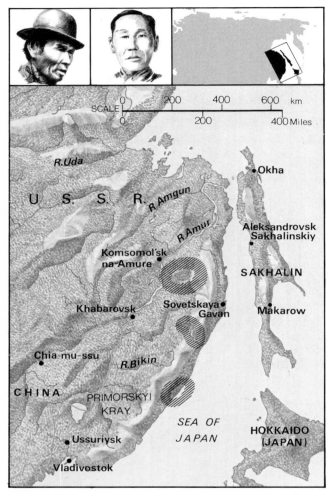

Since the Russian Revolution the lives of the Udege have permanently changed. Once they lived as a small isolated group of hunters, fishers and breeders of the spotted deer in the forested valleys of the wild Sikhote Alin mountain chain on the east coast of Russia, their only contacts being with Chinese traders. Indeed they still practise their old skills – hunting precious furs, fishing and breeding the spotted deer for its velvet antlers, which are supposed to have peculiar properties, and ferreting out the ginseng root, an important element of Chinese medicine believed to be a potent aphrodisiac. But they are no longer isolated, no longer dependent on Chinese trade, and no longer either independent or restricted in the means available to make a living. Now they live and work on collectives.

The Chinese traders undoubtedly cheated the Udege when they bartered with them for valuable furs, ginseng and velvet antlers, all luxury commodities highly prized in China. By 1937 every one of the widely scattered Udege groups was settled in collectivized villages. But,

reported the Soviets, 'the reorganization of the old economic order' was only achieved after 'a long and bitter struggle'. After initial resistance (there were only 1,357 Udege in 1926 – now there are only about 1,400) the old ways of the Udege were to change irrevocably.

'Reorganization of the old economic order' has meant that they still hunt – and hunting animals for their furs is still important to them – but their ancient skills have been supplemented by modern techniques and equipment. As well as catching sable by the old methods of traps and nets they now use guns supplied by the government. To increase and protect the supply of sable the Soviet government in 1950 strictly forbade sable hunting, permitting only Udege hunters to take 200 sable. And Udege mastery of hunting has not escaped official recognition. They have been rewarded for their skills by testimonials from the Ministry of Procurements. Production of precious ginseng is now organized by state enterprises. Large quantities of the valuable root are made available to the government by collective brigades. Before the Soviet period the Udege did not fish on the open sea. Their primitive boats had no sails. The Russians have taught them to use seine nets.

The Russians have also encouraged the Udege to develop agriculture and produce their own vegetables, especially potatoes. The 'Krasnyy Udegeets' collective farm succeeded in this new form of farming by producing wheat, rye, barley, oats, maize, soya as well as potatoes and other vegetables. The Udege who live in the south of Primorskiy Kray, who have been strongly sinicized and are known by the Chinese name of Tazy, have, however, for a long time grown tobacco and vegetables in their small patches of garden. These plots have now developed into large agricultural artels – collectively worked, profit-sharing associations – producing grain and vegetables with the aid of tractors and combines. They also have some cattle farms.

In the old days, before the Revolution, Udege affairs were managed by a council of elders chosen from the most experienced men of the group. All the profits and booty from hunting were shared by the whole settlement. In this way each family was well provided for during the long absence of the men on hunting expeditions. Like most of the people of the region, both men and women wore a tunic or robe made of fish-skins. By the end of the 19th century these were largely of Chinese cotton.

The creative spirit of the Udege flowered in many forms. They are talented story-tellers with a great store of tales and legends. The sun, in their mythology, was a woman whose love was sought by the moon. They made realistic sculptures in wood, bone and metal. These had a religious purpose and represented figures of animals and people. Udege embroidery reached a high level of design and finish and their clothes were beautifully embroidered in brilliant colors. They decorated domestic utensils and baskets made of bark with colored fretwork.

Udege divide their time between fishing and hunting. Cotton materials have replaced the clothes made of salmon, carp and other fish skins.

Music is only one of many Udege arts. They are talented sculptors, basket-weavers, embroiderers, and story-tellers with a vast store of legends.

The Udege boat is hollowed out of the trunk of a newly felled poplar. One boat can carry an entire family and its belongings to a new home.

The Soviets have suppressed the ancient Udege beliefs, which were traditionally animist and shamanist. The Udege revered the spirits of the woods, the marshes and the elements and offered sacrifices to them. Their harsh environment made them fatalistic towards illness and death. People they believed to be fatally ill were left alone until dead and the graves of the dead were avoided so as not to disturb them. The bear, the most savage animal in their world, was their totem and was held in considerable awe. It had a dominant place in their rites and when a hunter killed a bear – which was only permitted in carefully prescribed conditions – a feast was held at which the bear's head was eaten before the solemn ritual disposal of the body.

The smoky cold huts in which the Udege used to live have been largely replaced by log houses. And the old type of storehouse on piles is seldom seen now. According to Soviet reports every Udegeets village has a national school. Boarding schools are provided for the children of the more isolated groups who are also cared for by the medical air service. The village settlements have a shop and a medical center.

The Udege's age-old illiteracy has ended and a special script has been devised by Soviet linguists for their Udegeytsy native language – of the southern (Manchu) sub-group of the Tungus-Manchu languages. The Udege people seem to be undergoing a rapid process of linguistic russification which might in time erode their separate ethnic identity. This emerges from information contained in the 1970 census which reported that only 54 per cent of the Udege regarded their native language as their own compared to 73 per cent in 1959.

105

Tuvintsi
Tuva Autonomous Oblast

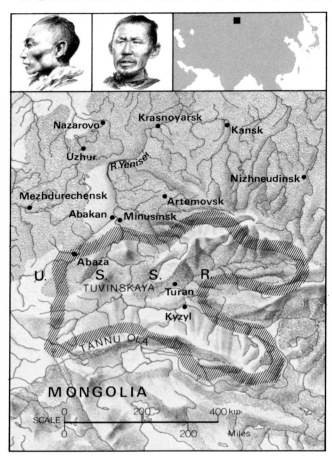

Some 700 years ago the region of Tuva in southern Siberia was a part of the Chinese empire. In those years, when the Mongol Yuan dynasty ruled China and an empire which extended across the greater part of the Asian world, it is unlikely that the people of the Tuva region thought of themselves as an ethnic unity. Today we call them the Tuvintsi and although they do not all share the same way of life, they do share a history. In their lands these people have absorbed Turkic, Mongol, Samoyed and Kettic speaking invaders, as well as people of the Altaic tribes to the west. Over the centuries, the Tuvintsi have been welded together as one Turkic-speaking people. And now all but 4,000 of the 139,000 Tuvintsi live in what is called the Autonomous Oblast of Tuva.

The region of Tuva borders on north-western Mongolia. It is a land of wide climatic extremes, burning summers and freezing winters. And it is also a land of geographical extremes. The wet northern parts skirt the Sayan mountains; the central steppelands are dry; and the high southern parts border on the arid wastes of Mongolia. Although from place to place the way of life of the Tuvintsi does vary today, before a process of

sovietization and collectivization took place the people followed even more varied ways of life. Some were hunters, fishermen or gatherers. Others were agriculturalists and grew grain crops. But the majority were nomadic pastoralists. In the northern parts they herded reindeer; in the drier south they herded cattle, horses, camels and even yaks. They moved with the seasons, in search of pastures rich enough to support their herds. Few could stay for long in one place.

In summer the reindeer herders drove their herds as far as 60 miles into the mountains, returning to the winter valley camps in September. They would then ride back into the mountains to hunt reindeer over three years old. Reindeer were mated in October and November and some were castrated. The young were born in April. Calves were kept tethered near the *yurt* (tent) all day long, and their mothers were milked three times a day. At night the calves and their mothers were allowed to wander freely. They usually returned to camp by themselves but in bad weather they were rounded up by herders riding reindeer. Reindeer herders rarely cultivated any crops but confined themselves to gathering a number of edible plants and roots. These included the highly nutritious roots and tubers of the adder's tongue and the lily *(lilium martagon)*. These were boiled, dried and stored for the winter in sacks. As in Mongolia and Buriatia it was the women who gathered all the food. Tea was prepared from many different plants and herbs like rhododendron, wild roses and saxifrage. Milk, butter and salt were added to the boiling tea and then cereals were mixed in to make it more like broth or porridge than tea as it is known to us.

The nomadic pattern of cattle and horse herders was more varied and complex and similar to the nomadism of the Mongols. In some places they moved from the southern mountain slopes where they lived in winter to the river valleys in summer. In other parts they moved in quite the reverse direction. For all these nomads their herds provided meat and milk products. But life was always hard and hazardous because of the rigorous climate, the high mortality rate and the infertility of their stock. Hunting and fishing were necessary subsidiary occupations for the Tuvintsi, especially those living in the north. They hunted small animals like the sable and squirrel for their furs, and they also hunted larger animals – foxes, wolves and deer – with guns (which had been introduced from Mongolia) and bows and arrows.

From February to April Tuvintsi men on skis would hunt squirrel and sable and there were large collective hunts for deer. Between May and June there was little hunting, but in July large-scale collective hunts for the larger deer would again be organized. In August there was little hunting and at this time the Tuvintsi would collect the lily bulbs and other roots. As they moved in September to their autumn pastures, sable hunting began again and at the end of September they would begin to hunt squirrel. Squirrel and sable hunting continued into

Although Kyrtys Chash-ool is a shepherd on a collective farm he and his people remain close in spirit to the old rough nomadic ways of their fathers.

Heaps of stones, *obo*, mark spirit territory. Every traveler makes an offering of food, vodka, money or tobacco in thanks for safe passage through the land.

(Bottom) Tuvintsi women do all the food gathering and prepare the meals. Their clothes are strongly influenced by their Mongol neighbors.

The holiest place inside the *yurt* is directly opposite the door where shamanist images used to stand on elaborately carved and decorated chests.

November but as the month progressed first individuals and then groups would hunt large deer for winter meat. There was little hunting in December and January as the snow was too deep for the dogs. In spring and autumn they fished using nets and lines, or spears and guns.

It is clear that nomadic Tuvintsi had also practised agriculture from earliest times, since there are remains of elaborate and extensive irrigation works. These fell into disrepair and the need for irrigation was met by simply flooding the fields. But the field produce was never seen as anything more than a supplement to the produce gained from the herds. There were no settled Tuvintsi entirely dependent on agriculture. Agriculture has always conformed to the necessities of nomadic pastoral life.

Tuvintsi dwellings showed the influence of their long connections with Mongol culture which dates back many hundreds of years. Their *yurts* or tents were almost exactly the same as Mongol *yurts*. Tuvintsi made the felt

Though they no longer live in the conical birchbark tents, Tuvintsi still use them as work huts and for storage of food and clothes.

with which the *yurt* was covered by a long laborious process of heating, washing, and rolling wool. Inside, the *yurt* was arranged after the Mongol fashion with left and right hand sides reserved as the male and female areas respectively and the holiest place opposite the door. This pattern was also followed in the birch bark tents and wooden structures often used in the summer. Shamanistic images were placed opposite the door.

Shamanistic beliefs similar to those of the Altai, Buriat, Yakut and Mongols flourished until recently, although traditionally the Tuvintsi were also Buddhists. There were a large number of monasteries throughout the Tuva region. The cult of the *obo* played a large part in Tuvintsi religious life. An *obo* is a heap of stones placed on high passes and marking the boundary of territories said to be under the protection of the priests of the *obo*. As a man passed an *obo* he was supposed to make a sacrifice of money, vodka, food or tobacco to them as thanks for passing safely through their territory. The *obos* were also the sites of periodic festivals conducted by Buddhist lamas and attended by both men and women, in contrast to shamanistic ceremonies. The festivals honored and placated the *obo* spirits who were thought to control the natural conditions within their territory. These ceremonies were followed by games and feasting. All of these things reveal the varied influences which have contributed to the rich history of the Tuvintsi.

According to Chinese chronicles the area was ruled by Turkic Khanates between the 6th and 8th centuries. Evidence of their language is found throughout the region on stone inscriptions. It is a language related to present-day Tuvintsi but it is unlikely that they thought of themselves as an ethnic entity as the Tuvintsi now do. In 840 AD the Turkic or Uighur khans were defeated by the Yenisei Kirghiz whose dominance lasted until the 10th century. Many of the Uighur migrated to Tibet. Early in the 13th century the Tuvintsi fell under the domination of Genghis Khan, with important consequences for their later development. When the Mongol Yuan dynasty was established in China the Tuva became part of the Chinese empire and military detachments were established there, supported by military farming settlements which imported Chinese agricultural techniques.

The fall of the Mongol dynasty in China caused the division of the Mongols into eastern and western branches, and the Tuvintsi became dependent on the western Mongols or Oriat. The Altai state collapsed in the early 17th century due to internecine strife among the surrounding Mongols and so Tuva became part of the Dzhungariyan state under the Oriat khans. This state covered the entire Sayan-Altai Plateau. It lasted until the middle of the 18th century, during which wars and feuds caused the Turkic-speaking tribes and clans to divide and intermingle. After the fall of this state the Altai tribes were included in the Russian empire, while the Tuvintsi and other Sayan people joined the Manchu empire.

Under Manchu rule Tuva was governed as a distant province of China with a feudal structure and administration. Certain parts of the territory were given over to Mongol princes in return for their help in the campaign. The feudal lords owned the nomads' territories and pasture and the *arats,* or serfs, who were attached to them. Monasteries and religious institutions were established all over Tuva with the introduction of lamaistic Buddhism. At this time Russia and China were competing in Tuva. Russians began settling there from the beginning of the 19th century. Chinese officials were a great burden on the country and the Tuvintsi peasants seem to have been drawn towards Russians, while Tuvintsi feudal lords were drawn to the Chinese. This ambivalence is reflected in the words of the traveler F Kon at the end of the 19th century: ' . . . while Russia dressed the poorer peoples, China supplied material for the clothes of the rich.'

As the Chinese empire decayed, rebellions broke out in Tuva. From 1912 onwards when the Chinese empire collapsed, Tuva was in a chaotic state with feudal leaders hoping for alliance with Mongolia while a minority hoped to gain and consolidate power by calling for the help of Tsarist Russia. This was successful and plans were made for turning Tuva into a Tsarist colony. But after the Russian revolution in 1917 the situation became yet more confused as Tuva was embroiled in the Civil War. White Guards and Interventionists held the same territory. In 1921 with the help of the Red Army these were defeated and the Tano-Tuvinian People's Republic was established. This state was separate and independent of the Soviet Union while conducting international relations under its protection. The republic continued until August 1944 when its parliament addressed a request to the Soviet Union for the incorporation of the Tuva Republic into the Soviet Union. This was granted in October 1944 when the Supreme Soviet agreed to the request that Tuva was to become an Autonomous Oblast of the Russian Soviet Federation of Socialist Republics.

Incorporation within the Soviet Union has brought many changes. Universal education has been introduced, people have been settled on collectives to raise their animals on improved pastures and to engage in the more intensive agriculture which has been made possible by systematic irrigation and new crops. In the remoter regions where transport is difficult all Tuvintsi have now been collectivized, but the traditional pastoralist economy still predominates. The state guarantees prices for the furs and meat produced there. It would seem that as pastures and techniques of animal husbandry are improved, and agriculture developed, the Tuvintsi will increasingly relinquish their nomadic way of life and become settled agriculturalists and stockbreeders on the collective farms.

Evenki
Siberia

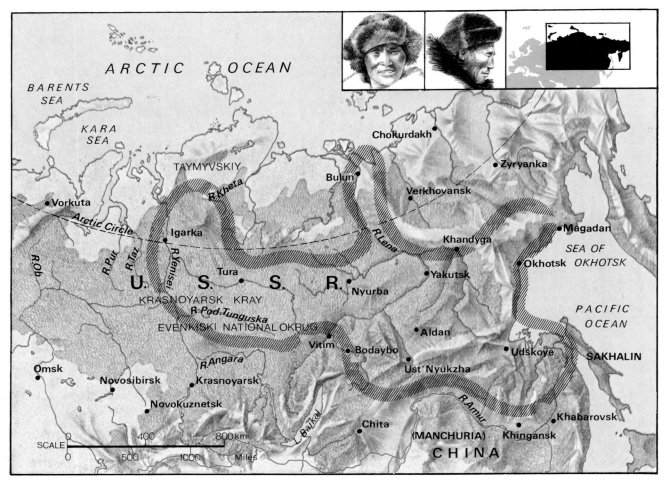

The Tungus, or Evenki as they have been called since 1917, have had many tributes paid to their honesty, intelligence and other attractive qualities by ethnologists and travelers who visited them in the pre-Revolutionary years. 'The Tungus do not steal' was the unanimous verdict. They were noted for their good humor and quick-wittedness and for the fund of folk-lore and legend which had been transmitted orally from one generation to another. The Tungus were then an illiterate people. The affection given by both men and women to children and the liberal attitude of the men to their women folk also came in for praise. The Tungus were reputed to be exceptionally magnanimous in armed struggles. They were known never to strip their opponents of their possessions or to harm them when victorious. Old men, women and children of the defeated tribe were allowed to go free. Predatory wars were unknown.

They are historically among the best known and most distinctive of the many groups of native peoples who live in northern Siberia and the Russian far east. They are now scattered over a wide area that stretches from where they live most compactly – north and south of the Arctic Circle in the Krasnoyarsk Kray – through Transbaikalia to Yakutia and the shores of the Pacific Ocean. From the 17th to the 19th centuries, largely due to the combined pressures of the Russians, Mongols and Yakut, the northern Tungus wandered far afield leaving their old familiar camping grounds for new places where they had never been before.

Because of Yakut pressure on their best hunting grounds and to escape the Russian tribute gatherers, a small group of Reindeer Tungus crossed the Sino-Russian frontier into north-western Manchuria in the 19th century, where they scattered over a huge expanse of territory and developed differences in their dialect, custom and clan structure.

The Tungus' first contact with the Russians came when the Cossacks, advancing from western Siberia, reached their tribal homelands in the early 17th century. They strongly resisted these intruders. They were incensed by the severity of the tribute in furs that the Cossacks imposed on them. In 1613 they were defeated by the

Olga, the talented shamaness of her Evenki clan is also its natural leader. She has a special costume and drum and is assisted by her husband.

Evenki Siberia

Traditionally shamans are not allowed to touch their own clothing. Olga's husband, Nikolai, helps her dress for a ceremony.

Though shamanism has lost much of its power since the Revolution and shamans are hounded by the government, they are still loved and obeyed.

Russians who were much better armed than they. By 1623 all Tungus within reach of the tax gatherers were paying their fur tribute to the Tsar. Clashes between Tungus and Russians continued sporadically against the Russian administration's oppression and the rapacity of the traders.

Before the Soviet Revolution, the northern Tungus were entirely nomadic. They wandered in the taiga and tundra with their herds of reindeer, adapting themselves to their environment with remarkable skill. From the raw materials at hand they fashioned most of the articles they needed for their domestic use and for their livelihood with a high level of craftsmanship and beauty. The men made things from wood, bone and metal and constructed boats and sledges with great expertise. The women dressed the skins from which all Tungus clothes were made and embroidered them artistically with beads and animal sinews. They wore warm fur clothes next to their skin with a fur hat. Their main occupation was hunting the valuable sable and ermine. They were renowned for their feats of marksmanship and for the dexterity with which they tracked and trapped wild animals.

They lived in *chum*. These were conical huts made from the poles of young larch trees stripped of their branches which could be swiftly erected and dismantled as they

112

To the Evenki the reindeer is not just a source of vital supplies of meat and dairy products; it is also a beast of burden—and a friend.

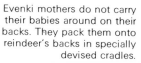

Members of several families take the reindeer to a trading post on the Argun river, leaving women with small children and old men behind.

Evenki mothers do not carry their babies around on their backs. They pack them onto reindeer's backs in specially devised cradles.

moved from camping ground to camping ground in search of new pastures for their reindeer. It was the Tungus women who had the all-important task of packing and unpacking the family belongings on the reindeer. Installed in the *chum* the women looked after the children and prepared the food. Their usual diet was of meat and salted fish with wildfowl and berries which, in season, abounded in the taiga. As the Tungus had never practised any form of agriculture they knew nothing of bread until they came in contact with the Russians when they learned the art of baking from them. But they also evolved a special type of unleavened bread said to be of excellent flavor, made in a frying pan before an open fire in the middle of the *chum* or in summer in outdoor ovens made of large stones.

Every Tungus was proud of belonging to his own Tungus clan and submitted to its rulings. Over the centuries the Tungus had evolved a high level of social relations based on the clan organization and its functions. Among the more important questions which the clan decided were marriage – regulated according to the customs and principles of exogamy, which compelled a man to marry outside his own clan – and all questions, embodied in customs and regulations, vendettas and

inter-clan problems, regarding the clansmen's morality. Among these so-called 'primitive' people, people who tried to intermix their own personal interests with those of their clan were considered 'bad people', however rich and otherwise worthy of esteem they might be.

Before the Revolution the Tungus were shamanists and animists who believed in the powers, for good or evil, of the spirits who inhabited trees and rocks. Each clan was strongly under the influence of its individual shaman. They consulted them over every problem, especially sickness. Consultations would be met with trances and spectacular performances by which the shamans were believed to be able to communicate with the all-powerful spirit world on behalf of their clients. The efforts of Russian Christian missionaries among the Tungus in the 17th-18th centuries bore little fruit. Although by 1862 some 9,480 Tungus were registered as Christians, most seem to have been nominal converts. The Tungus were too strongly under the shamans' influence to relinquish their traditional beliefs for Christianity.

At local seasonal fairs the Tungus bartered their valuable furs for iron and copper pots and pans, needles, scissors, flour, tobacco and other goods. They were said to have been cheated in these exchanges by unscrupulous 113

Evenki muffle their slender spruce skis with fur so they can pursue their fur-bearing prey like sables and ermines without making a sound.

Before moving on, Evenki roll up their birchbark tent coverings and sharpen long handled knives to cut through the taiga and spear bears.

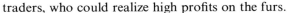

traders, who could realize high profits on the furs.

Throughout the 19th century and up to the fall of Tsardom, Tungus and Russians alike rapaciously over-hunted the best fur-bearing animals. The precious sable, for example, suffered so severely that it was virtually exterminated and the government was obliged in 1912 to encourage restocking it. Compared to the Russians the Tungus showed a superior attitude to their environment. Russian hunters were said to kill every animal they met, but the Tungus did not kill females or their young. The Tungus never left firewood burning when moving camp. Russian gold miners, on the other hand, burned Tungus forests to thaw auriferous river deposits.

As a result of the 1917 Soviet Revolution the traditional Tungus way of life, and the class structure on which it rested, had by the mid 1920s been completely swept away. The Tungus were thereafter known as the Evenki. The creation of the Evenkiski National Okrug in 1930 among the most compact group of Evenki in the northern Krasnoyarsk Kray in northern Siberia signified the passage of much of the old nomadic-tribal way of life to a new Soviet Socialist type of administration.

The intrinsic qualities of the Evenki continued to attract admiration. One observer reported in *The Listener* in 1936:

'Smallpox and alcohol have reached the Evenki through trade and thinned their numbers, so that today less than thirty families remain, or an average of about one person to every fifty square miles! But the traditional Tungus culture they brought with them from the north survives intact in the isolation of their natural stronghold. The old crafts flourish and beautifully fashioned objects decorate their tents, and, when they move are packed on their faithful reindeer. Human relationships are kindly and gentle and conversation is enlivened by a ready wit. If they tire of one scene, they can shift camp at will. To the harassed modern citizen of an overcrowded land their life seems like a utopian dream that should, at all costs, be preserved.'

The new Soviet socialist order in the Evenkiski National Okrug nevertheless effectively eliminated the clan chiefs and disrupted the clan system which was the very basis of Tungus social organization. Shamanism became taboo and the once powerful shamans were either killed or hounded underground. Tungus lands were nationalized and their livestock, the roaming Tungus reindeer herds,

Evenki know how to make the
most of local raw materials,
making the things they
need out of wood, bone,
skins and furs.

When dismantling a temporary
village the Evenki, a friendly
and considerate people, leave
the frame of their tents
behind for others to use.

were organized in collective farms. These changes were only accomplished at the cost of a prolonged struggle between the Tungus and the forces and agents of the Soviet government and were not completed until about 1950. They were carried out, in the official terminology, on the basis of 'voluntary socialization of Evenki properties'. One of the main elements in the propaganda campaign mounted by the Bolsheviks to influence the poorer Evenki in favor of their socialization aims was the class war. This was a concept which was alien to the traditional Tungus social structure in which there were relatively few differences between rich and poor. The Tungus chiefs were democratically elected and, in the all-important clan organization, of minor significance. But under the Soviet system all chiefs and better-off Tungus, who were probably in most cases the people's natural leaders, overnight became oppressors of the people. They were stripped of their power and property and were lucky if they escaped with their lives.

Having thus prepared the way for the Soviet socialist order, the Bolsheviks introduced more positive economic, educational and public health measures with a view to the 'liquidation of the age-old backwardness and darkness' of the Evenki. These negative epithets concentrate on illiteracy and pre-industrial stages of economic development according to Marxist criteria of progress. They do no justice to the actual lively social development of the Evenki at this time.

Early on the Soviets started an energetic campaign to overcome the Evenki's almost complete illiteracy. The first stage of this literacy campaign centered round the *Kul'tbasa*, or Cultural Base, established in Tura in 1927. This many-sided institution engaged in elementary teaching in literacy and also contained a veterinary post, a dispensary and a bath-house. It was also used as an information center to disseminate basic ideas about the Soviet system and its advantages for the Evenki. The first boarding school for Evenki children was established at about the same time. It met with little favor among Evenki parents, who were suspicious of this unusual separation from their children.

As, before the 1917 Revolution, the Evenki had no written language Soviet scholars devised an alphabet to create one. The first book printed in Northern Tungus appeared in 1928. This was followed by an increasing flow of printed Evenki school books and an expanding network of schools. By 1970 the Evenki were officially declared almost entirely literate.

The Soviet government intervened energetically to stamp out endemic Evenki diseases such as tuberculosis, trachoma and smallpox and their formerly high infant mortality rate. According to Soviet sources, this campaign bore fruit in a great reduction in infant mortality and the disappearance of anti-sanitary ways in Evenki life, through instruction given in local medical centers.

The population in the Evenki Okrug has, despite these 115

Evenki Siberia

This sea-otter hunter once
would have shared his catch
among his clan by custom.
Now he hunts on a
cooperative basis by law.

Before animal skins can be used to make things they have to be treated. These children are watching a skin-smoking frame being assembled.

(Bottom) Clothes made from slowly smoked, stretched skin are soft, supple and finally beautiful when decorated with beads and animal sinews.

Safe from the teeth of hungry rats precious winter clothes are stored along with the grain high up in barns like this.

measures, remained more or less stationary over some decades. The population, according to the all-Union census of 1970, was 13,000 and indicated a small increase over the 10,000 at the time of the previous census in 1959. Although regarded as the strongest of the people of the north, the Evenki were never a numerous people. They were always thinly spread over a huge area.

There have been many changes in the traditional basis of the Evenki economy and way of life since the reindeer herds were collectivized. With collectivization came settlement in Russian-type houses for this formerly nomadic people. And since about 1947, according to Soviet writers, the old methods of hunting for fur-bearing animals have been reinforced by fur-farming, especially of silver-black foxes, which is now carried on in almost all collective farms. Agriculture has been introduced in the south of the Evenkiski Okrug. Oats, barley, vegetables and potatoes are now grown by Evenki, a people who formerly never practised any agriculture. The diet of the Evenki, once almost entirely based on meat and fish, is now in some places enlivened by home-grown and farm products, as well as bread which has been familiar to them for some time.

117

Buriat
Buriat-Mongol ASSR

Buddhism brought masked lamas to dance in the Buriat *tsam* festival, but the ancient shamanist spirits — reindeer, bird and death's-head remained.

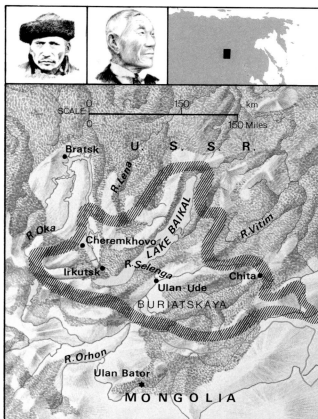

The Buriat are the northernmost of the Mongol peoples. Their physical type, dialect, economy and many of their customs are similar to those of the central group of Mongols. But the question of their origin has caused great controversy. Some scholars maintain that they are descendants of Turkic tribes living to the west of Lake Baikal – perhaps related to the Orkhon Turks – with a later Mongol admixture; others say they are descendants of successive waves of Mongols who arrived in the Baikal areas from the south. Buriat themselves shed little light on this question. One group of clans living west of Lake Baikal claim to be descendants of a grey bull. And another group who live east of the lake trace their ancestry to a female swan who, they say, came down from heaven, took off her feathers to bathe in the lake and was captured by a hunter who made her his wife.

Whatever their origins the Buriat only formed relatively recently as a people. They did not exist at the time of Genghis Khan, although several of the tribes which came to make up the Buriat did. In the 18th century some of these tribes were forced into temporary unity against the advance of the Khalkha Mongols. Some also united against the Russians when they expanded through Siberia. But at this time the Buriat who then had no centralized system of government and no great war leaders soon realized that independence for them as a 119

Buriat Buriat-Mongol ASSR

As the old nomadic ways
ended and the Buriat settled to
herd cattle for the new Russian
settlers, their felt *yurts* were
replaced by wooden huts.

This rich Buriat family of the
1880s owned many sheep,
goats and especially horses
which were highly prized and
often sacrificed to the gods.

This woman is poor but she has a child and knows that after death her soul will rest. Women who died childless became vengeful evil spirits.

Russian trade goods – guns, tools and clothes.

In the east however, the Buriat were less influenced by the Russian newcomers. The sandy steppes in their region were unsuitable for agriculture and this discouraged the Russian peasants from settling there. While in the west the Buriat began to live in wooden houses and to wear Russian dress, in the east many continued to live in their Mongol-type felt tents moving several times a year and to wear the national long-belted robe.

The Buriat were divided into four clans. The Khori, the largest, descended from the legendary Swan Daughter of the Sky, lived in the east. In the west lived the Bulagat and Ekhirit who both claimed descent from the mythical bull, Bukha-Noyon. And in the south lived the Khongodor people, said to have come from Mongolia.

Although each clan was associated with ancestral shrines and holy places and although the divisions of the clans, which consisted of the descendants of particular ancestors, were allotted their own territories by the Russians, the four clans were not territorial units. These lineages often grew too numerous for the land the Russians allocated to them – much of it in any case was taken by Russian settlers – and large numbers of people migrated eastwards to find new pasture. Thus in the 18th century the western Buriat settled the Selenga and Barguzin valleys east of Lake Baikal and during the 19th century the Khoril moved in successive waves to the Aga Steppe. At the same time there arrived groups of people in flight from wars and famines in Mongolia who took any free land they could find in the Baikal area. They usually settled among the original Buriat. The settlement pattern was consequently immensely complicated.

The Russian administrators continued to demand of the senior man in the lineage that he collect tax and other dues from his kinsmen. By the 19th century he had to journey hundreds of miles to seek out all his kinsmen, and he also had a large number of people living on his land who were not his kinsmen at all. At the end of the century the Russians made drastic proposals for land reform which threw the Buriat into dismay. They planned to give everyone, irrespective of whether they were settlers or old inhabitants, identical rights to land. This meant that the Buriat who herded horses, sheep and cattle extensively would have no more land than peasant farmers who needed only a small, cleared area for fields. It was one element in a complex political situation which was later to make the Buriat revolt.

At the end of the 19th century the Buriat had two religions. The Buriat who lived east and south of Lake Baikal had long been Buddhists. The people who lived west of the lake remained, despite Russian attempts to convert them to Orthodox Christianity, shamanists.

Shamanism is any religion in which the main specialist role is played by a shaman. A shaman is someone who is able to control his mind and body in such a way as to reach an ecstatic trance state during which he believes, and can

group was impossible. They chose to subjugate themselves to the Russians.

Under the Russian system of indirect rule the Buriat continued to live much as they always had. It was not until the beginning of the 20th century that they underwent important changes. At this time they numbered about 210,000 and lived to the west, south and east of Lake Baikal, and southwards and eastwards into northern Mongolia, Dauria and also in north Manchuria.

The Buriat were nomadic pastoralists. They kept cattle, sheep, goats and horses. Like all Mongols they prized the horse above all other animals. They thought the best milk and most delicious meat and fat came from the horse. All through the summer they sacrificed them to the gods creating occasions for gluttonous feasting.

When the Russians set up towns in Siberia they required meat and preferred beef. The Buriat responded to this demand by increasing their cattle herds and preparing winter fodder. They consequently became less nomadic. They even adopted new agricultural methods from the Russian peasant farmers who flocked into the fertile valleys west of Lake Baikal and became dependent on

121

This old woman lives at
Ulan-Ude on the trans-Siberian
railway, which opened Buriat
territory to crowds of
land-hungry Russian settlers.

The western Buriat were the
first to be affected by Russian
peasant settlers as their land
was rich and fertile. They
soon adopted Russian ways.

22

make others believe, that he is possessed by a spirit or
that he is on a journey to an invisible underworld or
heaven. The shamanism of the western Buriat was one
of the most complex and developed of northern Asia.

The western Buriat shamanists believed that the cosmos
had several layers: the heavens, the air, the earth and the
underworld. The ultimate source of all life and power
was the heavens, called *tengri*, which was conceived of as
symbolically male, as a father. The earth, on the other
hand, was impure and uncreative, female, and called
mother or old woman. The idea of *tengri* was also divided
into numerous kinds of skies: autumn-white-sky, dark-
blue-stormy-sky, yellow-sky, and so on. Each of these
skies was at the same time a physically existing type of sky
and a mythical personified deity who could help or harm
human beings. The Buriat believed that there were 99
tengri: 55 wise, benevolent white *tengri*, and 44 evil,
malevolent black *tengri*, who lived respectively in the
west and the east of the heavens. The elders of the clan
sacrificed horses, their heads pointing in the direction of
the relevant *tengri*'s dwelling place, and begged for
prosperity for their people in return for this addition to
the *tengri*'s herd.

Then the Buriat believed in numerous spirits who were
essentially the immortal souls of certain dead people:
shamans, powerful men, the suffering, criminals, suicides,
the wronged and women who died childless. These angry
souls became spirits and took their vengeance by harming
the living. The Buriat attributed almost all disease and
misfortune to them. The spirits were invisible to normal
people. They lived in any object or animal – trees, rivers,
dogs, mice, boxes – anything. It was only when people
lost their normal sight, when they were asleep and dream-
ing, when they were delirious, or hysterical, or in a trance,
that they were able to see where the spirits were hiding.
Shamans who were able to enter a trance state at will by
means of rhythmic drumming, shaking and dancing,
could discover where the harmful spirits were, find out
what sacrifice would placate them, and report to the
suffering people.

The spirits played two common tricks. They either
stole a person's soul from his body, causing weakness and
unconsciousness, or chose a human's body as their
dwelling place, thus taking charge of his mind. Such a
possessed person would have symptoms or physical
illness and would act in a manner completely unlike
himself. The psychological symptoms were very like
hysteria; all kinds of unconscious, repressed thoughts
and feelings came out under the guise of the words of the
spirit. Sometimes a spirit possessed whole crowds of
people among the western Buriat. They would sing, weep
and dance, moving from settlement to settlement, chanting a monotonous refrain in unison.

It was particularly these psychological disorders that
the shaman was able to cure. He specialized in luring the
spirit out of the patient and putting it into a specially

prepared model or idol called *ongon* where it could be induced to remain, by means of sacrifices and flattery.

There were black and white shamans who specialized in serving the respective black and white cycles of *zayan* and spirits. A white shaman wore white clothes and gave sacrifices of male, white-colored animals and foods such as milk and curds; he asked his spirit-helpers to persuade the western *tengri* to bestow happiness and plenty. A black shaman, dressed in black, colored half his face with soot, and gave sacrifices by night of dark-colored female animals and black foods such as bloody meat. His task was more difficult and dangerous than that of the white shaman for he had to go to the evil spirit and trick it into giving up a soul without himself being harmed. To do this a black shaman would disguise himself as various animals or insects. People feared black shamans, because they were suspected of offering the soul of a person whom they disliked in exchange for the captured soul of the patient. This unfortunate enemy would then fall ill and die. The Buddhism of the eastern Buriat was not so very different from the shamanism of the western Buriat. Although the main beliefs and rituals had originated in Tibet by the time they reached the Lake Baikal area they had already been mixed with local Mongol ideas derived from shamanism. Thus, for example, while lamas would read the holy Tibetan books to obtain prosperity for the local population, the site of the ceremony was frequently a former shamanist shrine and the deity addressed was only a re-named version of one of the *zayan*.

For all its foreign origin, the Buriat took to Lamaist Buddhism with enthusiasm. By the 20th century there were 31 monasteries and approximately one in five Buriat men was a lama. With the establishment of monastery schools the level of education of the people was enormously raised. The monasteries taught at something like the western university level, with degrees in philosophy, logic, astrology, anatomy and medicine. The monasteries also brought a high standard of carpentry, painting, metalwork, and building to Buriatia. It may also be true that the population of east Buriat was morally strengthened. The western Buriat, at any rate, were noticeably more apathetic, more illiterate, more given to alcoholism, and more diseased than their Buddhist kinsmen.

It was at the beginning of the 20th century that the Trans-Siberian Railway reached Buriat territory, bringing with it crowds of land-hungry Russian peasants. In 1903 and 1905 the Buriat revolted against the new land law. Their leaders, young intellectuals from Russian universities and the Buddhist monasteries, attempted to create a national unity without great success. At the time of the 1918 revolution and during the Civil War they tried again. But the dilemma of the Buriat, the result of their uneasy position between the Russians of the west and the Mongols of the east, again resulted in a split which crippled the nation – although this time perhaps there was a new economic factor in their division.

123

Some Buriat claim to be descended from a gray bull. Other clans say their ancestor was a female-swan captured by a hunter while bathing.

Ket
Yenisei river, southern Siberia

To Russians in Siberia this is a new land. The endless taiga and tundra slowly reveals its secrets and becomes a land of the future with huge mineral resources and untapped power. But to the 1,200 Ket, a tribal people whose ways have changed little over a thousand years, who live in the thick forests and rocky hills close to the northern valley of the Yenisei river, Siberia is an ancient homeland. The ways of these old Siberians are those of the forest and the river, not of technology.

Until the new Siberians, the Russians, recently introduced collectivization and settlement programs the Ket were a seasonally nomadic people. Their yearly cycle had two main phases: migratory fishing in the summer, and hunting in the area surrounding a permanent camp in the winter. Hunting and fishing provided almost all of their needs, and anything else – things like guns and ammunition, flour and bread – came by way of trade with the Russian fur-traders who penetrated Siberia.

In April, when the snow begins to melt, the Ket would traditionally stop hunting and abandon the earth-covered houses of their winter camp. They set up birch-bark or reindeer-skin tents near the spring flood waters at the edge of the forests and near the smaller rivers. They began to fish and put their fish-weirs in order. They would also prepare their boats and fishing tackle and hunt wild fowl. Then, as the summer draws near, they would put their possessions in raised store-houses in the forest, and would all head downstream. Some traveled in small, light canoes, others in large craft called *ilimkas* which were like house-boats.

During this time food is abundant and they congregated in large groups. Wild fowl are easy to catch as the birds are then moulting, athough the Ket only hunted the cocks as it is also the breeding season. The fowl would be trapped, chased into large groups by dogs and then killed by the hunters' hands or shot with poisoned arrows. So many could be caught in this way that families might often eat six or seven meals a day. The birds left over could be stored for a week in deep pits.

Later in the summer, after the solstice, the Ket began fishing and gathering pine nuts in preparation for winter. They caught the fish in nets and weirs which direct fish into an enclosed area where they could be speared at leisure. To preserve the fish, they would be boiled, dried and smoked over a fire and then chopped up. This turns them into what in Siberia is generally called *pors*. It is stored in birch-bark boxes or small bags made of bird-skin. The Ket also collected fat by boiling duck-skins and fish intestines.

In September the Ket moved upstream to rockier regions, pulled up their boats and settled down. They began to build their winter earth houses and prepare their winter clothes. They also made slim wooden skis to use when the snows hardened, and broad skis covered underneath with skin from the feet of reindeer or horses to use when the snow was still soft. They hunted wild fowl, dried and froze them for the winter. From the middle of October until the beginning of January hunters would go out alone near their camps to hunt squirrels and other furry animals. The hunters would use traps, bows and arrows and guns. Squirrels were skinned and boiled by the wives, but only men were allowed to roast meat. And then during the period of intense cold which extends throughout January, the hunting ceased. The Ket lived on their stores and fish caught nearby.

February was the beginning of the great movement. The reindeer had been kept close to the settlement until this time. Now families set out on long hunting trips

When fishing, the Ket live in conical tents covered with sewn strips of treated birchbark which is both lightweight and waterproof.

(Above) When a Ket family travels the father leads the way in his own sled. Wife and children follow in sleds tied together with leather cords.

In winter the Ket drive elk and deer into the deep snow and capture them. Elk skin is processed and stretched, then used to make clothing.

(Bottom) The Ket hunt smaller animals, mainly squirrel, for their valuable fur. They set elaborate traps for them before it snows over.

with their tents, equipment and catch all piled on the sledges and pulled by the reindeer. The party would always go in a definite, fixed order. The head of the family went first in his sled, never carrying anything, showing the direction to be taken and 'opening the way'. He was followed by his wife in a different type of sled, and attached by cords to this were the children's sleds, the loaded sleds and finally the rest of the reindeer. On these trips the Ket hunted bear; and elk and deer were driven into deep snow where they could be easily killed. At the camping places the wives erected the tents, while the men collected firewood. When a man was hunting alone, he would dig a hole in the snow, line it with branches, light a fire and then fall asleep in it.

Every man and woman among the Ket looked up to a shaman as a kind of priest. The shaman's role passed down from a man to his daughter and through her to his grandson. Sometimes, however, a daughter would not take up the role, and it passed directly to the grandson. Within the pantheon of Ket gods and spirits it was the task of the shaman to communicate with the gods and to protect the community from malevolent spirits and the machinations of other shamans. One family in five would have a little shaman whose sole function was to tell stories. In the whole Ket community there were only 15 great shamans. Their functions included curing rituals and the spiritual protection of the group. They had great power and were accorded much respect. The entire group was involved in making their elaborate robes and providing them with a wand, a drum and headdress.

The Ket believed that every man had no less than seven souls, including one which was distinctive to man, giving him life and consciousness. These souls transmigrated within the clan and could also pass into bears. This goes some way to explain the respect the Ket gave to bears and the feast held to honor them after one had been killed. Any sickness in a man was thought to be due to an injury of the man's soul, or to a soul having been caught and eaten by the evil female deity, Khosedem. A shaman then had to free the man's soul by making Khosedem excrete or vomit. Death was put down to Khosedem eating the soul. And since she always excreted the soul after a while, it could then be reborn as a child of the clan. Ket mythology is still rich with mythical beings and themes, alive in everyday stories.

Today the Ket language is encouraged in the primary schools of modern Siberia, where so much else has changed for the Ket. There is now a general literacy among the people, and most Ket also speak fluent Russian. But the Ket are no longer nomadic. Today they do not move with the seasons or with their reindeer after bears. Instead they are collectivized, settled and hunt in brigades. They are fur farmers and large scale reindeer herders. But many of the Ket's traditional methods also remain, adapted to the new way of life that the Russians have brought with them to Siberia.

Nivkhi
Bureinskii Khrebet and Sakhalin

Nivkhi today are great tea
drinkers, but tea, as well as
rice, millet, sugar and salt
were only introduced to them
by Russian and Chinese traders.

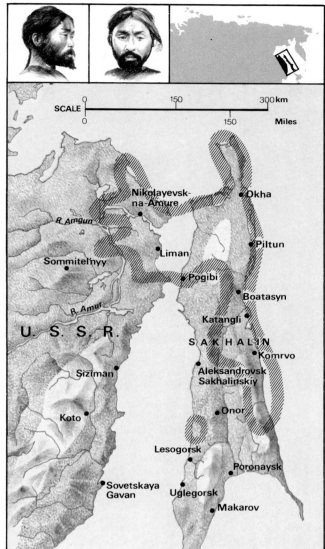

The Nivkhi – who were called the Gilyak before the
Russian Revolution – live on the lower reaches of
the Amur river and on Sakhalin. They are Paleo-
asiatics, numbering well over 4,000; the Nivkhi of the
lower Amur basin may well be the most direct descendants of the neolithic population in the area, though it is
not certain whether the Nivkhi of Sakhalin originated or
migrated there.

The Nivkhi were traditionally, and remain today,
fishermen and sea hunters. The most important fish for
them are salmon, beluga and sturgeon. They also catch
sea lions and seals in large fixed nets, or by harpooning
them on open water with a floating harpoon. The Nivkhi
also hunted bears, sables, otter, lynx and martens. Some
Nivkhi learned to plant potatoes in the mid-19th century. 127

In 1903 a Russian doctor
came to the island of
Sakhalin to vaccinate the
Nivkhi families there
against a smallpox epidemic.

Even before the Russians came they knew how to work
copper and silver inlay as well as having the normal skills
of smiths. Labor was fairly strictly divided. The men
hunted and fished and made the tools necessary for this.
Women processed fish and animal skins, prepared birchbark for various uses, sewed and decorated clothing,
made utensils, gathered plants, cared for the dogs and
managed the household.

Fish was and is the Nivkhi's staple food, especially
yukola or dried fish. Fish and seal fat was used extensively
and a favorite delicacy included fish skins, seal fat,
berries, rice and sometimes crumbled *yukola*. Raw fish
garnished with wild garlic was another favorite, and these
two dishes are still eaten today. Rice, millet and tea, with
small amounts of bread, sugar and salt have been used
by the Nivkhi ever since their first contacts with the
Russians and Chinese. They also eat dogs – their principal
draft animals – especially in the past during the bear
festivals, which have now fallen out of Nivkhi life.

The traditional Nivkhi sled was so narrow that the
rider wore skis while sitting astride it. Gradually, as carts
became more economic, larger sleds, drawn by 9 to 11
dogs, were adopted. They used two kinds of skis – bare
skis for short trips and fur-lined skis for long-distance
hunting expeditions. They traveled along rivers in light
hollowed boats of poplar which they propelled with oars
128 or poles. For longer distances they used a boat of three

This old man wears traditional
summer clothes—a richly
embroidered fur or fish-skin
robe over cotton pants with
a conical birchbark hat.

Each household in the fishing
and sea-hunting villages on
the mouths of spawning rivers
kept 30-40 dogs for fur and
meat as well as to draw sleds.

(Bottom) By tradition women
could be bought, sold and
turned out of their homes. In
childbirth they were abandoned
for days in cold, damp huts.

For long sled trips the men wore sealskin kilts as well,
and a fur hat with fur earmuffs. Today, in the central
settlements, most Nivkhi wear western clothes, although
women and old people stick to the old styles more than
men and boys. When old Nivkhi are buried, they are
dressed in native costume.

The Nivkhi clans were patriarchal, and practised strict
exogamy: men took brides not from clans to which they
gave their women, but from other clans. Most people
still follow the old rules of marrying outside the clan,
although in some villages there are marriages between
Russians and Nivkhi. Young people who go to the cities
to study or work rarely find their wives there, but either
marry before they go or return to the villages to marry.

The Nivkhi speak a language quite different from their
Tunguso-Manchurian neighbors' language, although
they borrow many words from these languages. The
number of Nivkhi who consider Nivkh their native
language is gradually dropping, and is already under half
the total population. The others speak Russian, though
a rather strange form of it, and all are at some dis-
advantage among Russian speakers. Before the Russian
Revolution the Nivkhi were officially Christian, but their
view of nature is animistic. They believe that all things
have their master. If a Nivkhi moves to a new place, he
must go into the forest nine days before leaving and
address the master of the earth. He asks him to let his
children prosper and his catch be a good one. This ritual
is also carried out when a son sets out for the city, and he
is given leaf tobacco to take with him as an offering to the
master of the place where he is going. Building a house is
also accompanied by a number of rituals, including placing pieces of flint or sweetbriar or a pike's head under the
post holes so that the evil spirits are kept out and prevented from doing any mischief. When the house is built
a special feast is held, and a dog is killed for each of the
four corners. The dogs' blood is smeared on them and the
flesh is eaten by the guests. The dogs' skulls are put up
on the top of the house to guard it. Very strict rules also
surround the hearth fire, which has to be lit by the oldest
member of each household. And whenever a member of
any clan moves away he is given a piece of the clan
steel for lighting his new fire. There is always 'a master of
the house' in the form of a special wooden idol which is
fed after every successful hunt, and on special occasions.
These idols are passed on in the male line. The Nivkhi also
make special armless idols in cases of sickness. Almost
all the small peoples of the north have similar idols.

The Nivkhi are clannish and only go to cities where
they have relatives already established. Few Nivkhi are
employed in industry. The reason is partly that enterprises are unwilling to hire them – Nivkhi like to take
time off to go fishing during the autumn salmon-run.
Gradually, however, Nivkhi are entering industrial and
lumbering trades – quite a change from the traditional
occupations.

wide cedar boards, the bottom board bent upward like
a spade.

Nivkhi villages were usually made up of just one clan
or family, living in about 20 houses, usually strategically
placed near the mouths of spawning rivers. In the 19th
century the Nivkhi on Sakhalin built dugout houses like
the Koryak ones, but from the Ming dynasty onwards
the dugouts were replaced by Manchu frame *fanzas*. A
fanza had a rectangular floor plan, a ridged roof and
flues under the sleeping benches to heat them. In summer
the Nivkhi moved to dwellings on stilts. The back of the
house was where everyone lived and the front was a storehouse. The house was also surrounded by storehouses
and racks for drying fish.

The traditional dress of the Nivkhi men is trousers
with a robe which fastens from left to right and reaches
to the knees. They wear this outfit with sealskin boots
and a conical birchbark hat. Women wear cloth or fish-
skin robes, longer than men's, and ornamented along the
edges with copper disks. In winter men and women wear
fur garments over their clothes, with the fur side outward.

Koryak
Kamchatka

The Kamchatka peninsula is a strange land of mighty mountains and live volcanoes. Its people are the Koryak. The largest group, who roam the interior, are nomadic reindeer herders. Their kinsmen who live on the coast are fishermen and hunters of sea mammals. The basis of their society was cooperation, on which their survival depended – not only cooperation with each other, but with the land and the animals and spirits who share it with them.

The men of each kin group hunted together and shared the kill equally between them. The animal's skin went to the man who had killed it. Before the people ate they fed the spirit who inhabited the place where the kill was

Koryak sacrifice dogs to the
evil spirits *kalau* to ward
off disasters and disease. They
are usually young or sick ones,
unfit to draw the sleds.

Anna Prokopyevna, a 95 year
old professional huntress,
has received the Red Banner
of Labor award. One year she
bagged 300 ptarmigan.

made so that their next hunt on that spot would also be
successful. Reindeer bones and horns were gathered up
and taken to sacred ancestral places to honor the
ancestral spirits. A bear was accorded special honor. Its
skull was placed in the hunter's tent. Cedar branches
were placed in its eyes, nose, mouth and ears and fat and
other items, depending on the bear's sex, were placed in
a grass basket. This basket was handed to a passer-by
who put on the bearskin and walked away while the
hunter shot at him with fake ammunition. Then the skull
was taken to the ancestral place and the skin given to the
hunter. The Koryak never killed a wolf if they could
avoid it, for they believed the wolf was their kinsman.

The 7,500 Koryak today are one of the Soviet Union's
'small peoples'. Until recently they lived in nine isolated
groups. Most of them now live in the Koryak National
Okrug on Kamchatka. The Soviets have made considerable efforts to diversify the economy by introducing fur
and poultry farming, vegetable gardening, hauling,
motorized fishing and more rational methods of reindeer
breeding. Kamchatka has experienced intense industrial
development over the last decade, especially with the
discovery of gold, and the fishing industry has become
more important. Koryak life has been much improved,
but as long as reindeer breeding remains an important
branch of the Soviet economy in the north, more will have
to be done to make the professions of reindeer-breeder,

132

To insure good hunting,
sacrificial dogs are impaled on
stakes driven into the snow
with their muzzles up and their
bellies turned toward the east.

hunter and fisherman attractive to the young.

Reindeer provided the nomadic Koryak with nearly everything they needed: meat, skins for clothing and tents, transport and thread made from the tendons. The Koryak moved several times each winter as pastures were used up. In April the really hard work began when pregnant does were separated from the rest of the herd to be given care and protection from predators. The herdsmen, helped by their families, worked on foot using lassos. When summer came the herd was driven to the mountains, to pastures close to fish-filled rivers. In September and October the herd returned to the main family camp for the autumn festivals, and with the first snows, were driven to winter pastures.

In spring the nomads were able to join their fishing kinsmen and help them prepare a stock of fish for winter. They also hunted sea mammals from the ice floes. The spring hunting season lasted from mid-March until the end of June. The autumn season lasted from mid-September until the end of November. Then the Koryak hunted from flat-bottomed boats with nets made from strips of sealskin. Legends printed in the 18th century say that the Koryak hunted whales with huge nets using stones for sinkers. The net was attached to a cliff while the hunters in their boats drove the whale into the net and killed it with a shower of spears. All the parts of the whale were useful and were sometimes traded with the reindeer Koryak. To catch smaller fish, the fishermen used a barrier and an underwater sacknet or an iron hook and a dipper net. The catch was cleaned and hung on special racks, then left to dry in the sun. *Yukola*, dried fish, was prepared by the women. Fresh fish was piled into a pit, covered with earth and left to ferment.

Both the nomadic and the coastal Koryak hunted foxes, wolverines, otters, hares and ermine for their fur. Sables were trapped in nets, foxes and small animals were caught in spring traps and hares and partridges were caught in nooses. Bears, wild reindeer, marmots and mountain sheep were hunted for meat. Women gathered edible roots, berries, grasses and fly agaric – a red-capped hallucinogenic mushroom used both in religious rites and simply to get pleasantly intoxicated. Grass was used to line boots and make mats and baskets.

Reindeer breeders lived in tents built by the women. They were cylindrical at the base rising to a cone at the top. The tent poles were covered with reindeer skin with the fur on the outside. The skin covering was smoked to make it waterproof. Summer tents were made of hide from which the fur had been removed. The size of the tent depended on the wealth of the family. Sometimes several families shared a tent, separated by skin canopies.

The coastal Koryak lived in semi-dugouts. The base was a large pit, three to four feet deep. Vertical logs forming an octagon reinforced the walls of the pit. Each corner of the octagon was joined by a beam at the top. Four main posts in the center held up the roof. This was made of flat planks laid over the beams. The outside and roof were covered with sods. In summer the dugout was entered through a corridor in the side, but in winter the entrance, which served as a window and smoke vent, was a hole in the roof. Inside, benches along three walls were covered with skins and a canopy. Each dugout might house 40 people. In spring they moved to huts on stilts.

The reindeer Koryak traveled quickly and easily across the snow by reindeer sled. A reindeer was harnessed to the left to act as a brace when the sled traveled downhill. Dogs were also used to pull a four-staved sled which was common throughout eastern Siberia. Ten to 12 dogs made up a full team, but in Soviet times few Koryak have been able to maintain that many dogs. River boats were made from hollowed-out logs. Two or more were joined together for sea travel.

Meat was and is the staple of the Koryak diet. Reindeer meat is boiled but marrow, tendons, gristle and kidney are eaten raw. *Yukola* and pickled fish and the meat and fat of seals, walrus and whales are eaten by the coastal people. Tea, flour and sugar were rare before the Revolution. The Koryak diet remains virtually unchanged, not least because of the difficulty of supplying the isolated peninsula. However, most children now spend much of the year in state-run boarding schools and the Koryak are slowly acquiring a taste for Russian food.

Reindeer provided much of the Koryak clothing. The skins of young deer are best. Other furs and skins were made into hats, mittens and decorations. Men wore a long, widesleeved fur shirt gathered with a thong at the neck, perhaps with a cowl or wide collar. Their trousers were of fur and their boots of suede. Women wore a fur overall or shirt much like the men's, but they decorated it with tassels and embroidery. Both men and women added a fur strip of a different color to the edge of the shirt. This was often decorated with mosaic and stylized animal designs. Until the age of six children wore a one-piece fur suit. A baby's suit had a flap in the back, tied at the waist, and into this moss or shavings were pushed to act as a diaper. The hood, worn by both sexes was edged with dog fur and, like the shirt and trousers, was sometimes made of strips of light and dark contrasting fur. These costumes have changed little for the 800 or so Koryak who migrate with their herds. Young people who live in the central settlements prefer western dress, but the traditional costume is the one best suited to the climate and Soviet authorities have expressed concern because native craftsmen are not being encouraged to make the traditional clothes.

The Koryak had a complex set of religious beliefs. As well as placating the spirits after the hunt, many of their rites included games such as dogsled racing. Custom decreed that the vanquished dogs had to be sacrificed, both to propitiate evil spirits and to ensure that only the best dogs were bred. The dogs' bodies were placed on stakes belly-up with the muzzle pointing toward the east, 133

Koryak Kamchatka

Ordinary trucks would not get far on Siberian roads. Furniture is delivered to reindeer breeders in the Tundra by cross-country tractor.

Traveling in spring can be perilous. As he crosses a fast-melting ice-bridge in Kamchatka, this traveler is in constant danger.

Children wear one-piece fur suits. Babies' suits have a flap at the back through which moss or shavings are pushed to act as diapers.

guarding the village against an epidemic.

In November or December the seal festival was held. It is still a big occasion but has now merged with the Soviet new year celebrations. A special porridge of seal fat, chopped fish and berries was prepared and each hunter set willow stakes round a fire – one stake for every seal he had killed. Pieces of wood shaped like seals were tied to the stakes with seaweed and the images were smeared with the porridge. The people then danced, mimicking seals to the beat of a drum. After the dance the images were burned as the hunter wished his dead seals a safe journey to the other world. A similar ritual was performed for bears and mountain sheep. After the burning divinations were made with pieces of rope to see how many animals there would be next year. The river spirit, too, had to be fed so that it would continue to supply fish. But the Koryak never killed more animals than they could eat; if they did the spirits would be angry at the waste and would withhold game. Ancestor spirits looked kindly upon the living and could even restore sick people to health but the world of the Koryak was also populated with other, hostile, spirits who had to be propitiated with sacrifices of food and tobacco. Shamans had a role in communal rituals but they were not essential to family rites performed in the tents.

In the past the Koryak burned the bodies of their dead. A cremation was witnessed in 1957 by the Soviet ethnographer I S Gurvich. The corpse was a very old lady whose relatives sat near her body lying on the floor. All night long they ate, drank and played dominoes (in place of the traditional Koryak games). In the morning the relatives carried the body to the appointed place, laid it on the pyre and then slit the hem of the corpse's garment to 'open the way', and killed a dog. No one there could tell Gurvich why, before the pyre was lit, they leapt off it, crowing and flapping their arms. Nor did they know why they returned home in single file leaving on the trail two crossed stakes which they brushed with larch branches. The hero of many Koryak folktales is a raven (just as in many American Indian tales), but young people are forgetting the old ways and engage in the old rituals from habit or to please their elders.

Archaic rituals linger on, but much has changed for the Koryak since the Revolution. Reindeer breeding is being developed as the best and most economical way to feed Siberia's growing population, but if modern techniques and veterinary science are to be introduced to build up the best herds, young Koryak will need new training. At present there are too few technical schools. Soviet policy for all the 'small peoples' including the Koryak, has been to train a native élite capable of governing the local population and of developing a native culture, 'national in form, socialist in content'. There are now Koryak writers, teachers, nurses, doctors and government workers. But there are still too few technicians capable of guiding the Koryak into the 21st century.

135

Glossary to the peoples of Siberia and Mongolia

One million or fewer would be a reasonable estimate of the number of Siberian tribespeople who survive in the Siberia of the 20th century. In this far northern land of endless taiga and tundra and frozen wastelands, once the Siberian nomads' undisputed territory, these people now constitute a mere three per cent of the total population. The rest are Russians.

The ways of these old Siberian tribespeople are also losing ground in the 20th century. Nomadism is not favored by an administration whose technology has overcome many of the awesome problems of survival in Siberia. Hunting, trapping, fishing and herding can no longer be left to individuals or small groups. The resources of Siberia have to be exploited to the full if the Russians in this land are to be fed. Hunters and trappers live and work in a collective.

In the taiga, game hunting collective farms are called *gospromkhoses*. They consist of a few dozen families, perhaps 50 or 100 labor units, who live together in settlements and, just like everyone else, have to fulfil annual plans and quotas. These plans include the hunting of tigers, bears, squirrels, deer and, above all, sable and stags. The furs from animals like sable were what first attracted the Russians to Siberia and at one time, in the Ussuri region alone, 300,000 sable were caught annually. But at that time, no more than 50 years ago, most of the fur-trappers were Chinese.

The 50,000 Chinese trappers have now gone. Siberian trappers have joined collectives called *kolkhoses* and today bring in only 50,000 or so sable furs a year. Today the Russians are anxious to point out that the Chinese trappers of yesteryear conducted an irresponsible exploitation of the animal wealth—now the collectives have a more responsible attitude.

The native Siberians still hunt deer in the taiga, especially in spring when they grow their new antlers. The antlers have for hundreds of years been credited with remarkable healing properties and the Soviet pharmaceutical industry extracts valuable medicines from stags' antlers. It was, however, the Chinese who originally discovered the antlers' curative powers and used them for medicinal purposes over 2,000 years ago. The rediscovery of Siberia in the 1950s and the monuments to the 20th century which have been thrown up in the last 20 years have not completely buried the past ways of life. And the threat to Siberia from China, just across its southern frontier, which troubled the Siberians' Tsarist rulers still haunts their Soviet equivalents today. There has long been the fear that Russia could not hold her Siberian and far eastern provinces against China's vast, expanding population. But the resources of the Siberians' region would have been opened up even without this threat. The huge potential was irresistible. Russians in their millions were, and still are, encouraged to cross the Urals from European Russia and settle in Siberia. A host of scientific and technical resources were set in motion to conquer the new land. And the Soviet Union today conducts the century's most impressive drive to open up and exploit a territory hitherto occupied by only a thin scattering of tribal nomads.

ALEUT *Population:* 400. Language group: Eskimauan-Aleutian. The Aleut live on the Komandarskiy islands, including Bering and Mering islands, in the Bering Sea. They were transported there by Russian fur traders around 1820. Many Aleut have emigrated and now live in the USA. Traditionally they are hunters and fishermen who eat mostly fish and meat. Today most work in a hunting and trapping collective farm. They hunt sea mammals, such as sea-lions, walruses, and whales. Today the modern ships and equipment on the collective fishing farms have replaced the stone, wood and bone weapons of the past. On land the Aleut hunt polar foxes and seals for their expensive fur. The women supplement the diet with wild roots and seaweed that they gather. Traditionally Aleut are divided into clans. The members of each clan live together in the same village and hunt in their own territory. The ancient national dress of the Aleut is a parka jacket made of birdskins. The Aleut practise shamanism.

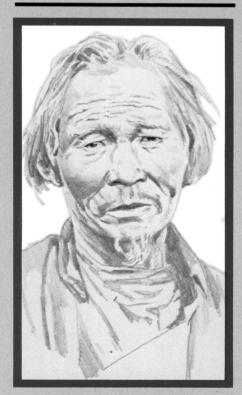

ALTAI *Population:* 55,000. Language group: Turkic. The Altai live mainly in the Gorno-Altai Autonomous Oblast in southern Siberia. They are divided into two groups: the northern Altai, consisting of the Tubula, Chelkan and Kumandin and the southern Altai consisting of the Altai proper, the Telengit, Telesi and Teleut. Traditionally the Altai are nomads, herding horses and cattle. Once most households had small barley plots which they tilled with wooden plows. In the north hunting was the main occupation. Nowadays most of the farming is done within the collective farm system, but open pasture farming is still practised in mountainous areas. Altai settlements are usually spread out over vast areas and are sparsely populated. Their dwellings are often made of poles and planks covered with birchbark. Altai society has traditionally been strongly male-oriented. Women became the property of their husbands and were considered unclean and potentially dangerous. The Altai are shamanists. They believe the world to be populated by good and bad spirits. One feature of their cult was the sacrifice of a horse to either Ulgen, the highest deity, or to Erlik, the evil master of the underworld.
(pages70-73)

ALYUTORTSI see KORYAK

APUKINTSI see KORYAK

BIRCU see EVENKI

BURIAT *Population:* 313,000. Language group: Mongolian. The Buriat live mostly in the Buriat-Mongol ASSR, around Lake Baikal in southern Siberia. Included in the tribe are the Tunka Soyot who are Tuvintsi (q.v.) by descent, but have adopted the Buriat way of life. The Buriat are mainly pastoral herders. They keep cattle, sheep, goats and a few camels, but value horses above all. The collective farms have brought about the settling down of the once nomadic Buriat, but besides farming they also hunt squirrels, sables, ermine, stags, bears and wolves, for both their meat and their fur, although their main diet is of dairy products. They hunt with guns, traps and snares, and also by shooting arrows from horseback and even poisoning bait with strychnine. Many Buriat are expert blacksmiths and make their own hunting implements. Others are skilled tanners and saddlemakers. Buriat dress is particularly beautiful. Their elaborate robes and skirts are supplemented with home-made jewelry. Shamanism was the ancient Buriat religion, but has been replaced by Buddhism. Buriat believed that the mountains, forests, rocks, sky and fire all possessed their own 'master' spirits, which could be good or evil depending on how they were treated. They celebrate an important annual festival of archery, wrestling and horseback riding.
(pages 118-123)

CHARCHUVEN see KORYAK

CHELKAN see ALTAI

CHUKCHI *Population:* 14,000. Language group: Paleo asiastic. The Chukchi live almost entirely in the extreme north-east of the USSR. They consist of two distinct groups: the coastal hunters whose basic occupation is hunting sea-mammals, such as walruses, whales and seals, and the nomadic reindeer breeders who live in the tundra. The two groups are linked by kinship and trade relations. For the sea hunters seals provided most of their needs: meat for their food, skins for clothing and footwear and in their houses. For the tundra nomads the reindeer did the same. Inland Chukchi camps consisted of a

137

number of tents, usually standing in line from east to west according to the wealth of the owner. Nowadays most live on modern collective farms. The Chukchi have an interesting system of counting, which is based on the number 20, the total of all fingers and toes. Their word for 'count' literally means 'to finger' and '20' means '20 fingers'. The Chukchi traditionally believe the entire universe is inhabited by spirits. Evil spirits spend their time hunting human souls. When they succeed, a man becomes ill or misfortune comes to him. To prevent this the Chukchi make sacrifices to the spirits of reindeer and dogs.

ENTSI see NENTSI

EVENKI *Population:* 25,000. Language group: Tunguso-Manchurian. The Evenki used to be known as Tungus. They include the Orochen, Bircu and Manegri. Evenki are scattered throughout Siberia from the Ob'-Irlish watershed in the west to the coast and Sakhalin in the east, and to Lake Baikal and the Upper Tunguska river in the south. A few live on the Iro and Orion rivers in the Mongolian People's Republic. The Evenki are divided into two groups who live differently in different places. The hunting and reindeer-breeding Evenki live in northern Siberia. The larger group of pastoral Evenki who keep horses and cattle also do some arable farming and hunting, and live in the southern Transbaikal. The northern Evenki hunt elk, reindeer, bears, squirrels, foxes and other fur-bearing animals. Fishing is only important to those Evenki living on the Okhotsk sea coast and around Lake Baikal. Evenki use sleds and skis to travel on the snow. They enjoy domestic occupations such as sewing and embroidering, carving articles from birchbark and blacksmithery. They frequently wear embroidered kaftans and suede boots. According to Evenki religion, everything has a spirit. They believe in an upper and a lower world. It is the shaman who protects his people from evil spirits.
(pages 110-117)

EVEN *Population:* 12,000. Language group: Tunguso-Manchurian. The Even are scattered throughout north-eastern Siberia including the Okhotsk coast. They are reindeer breeders and hunters. Formerly nomadic, they are now based on collective farms. Along the Okhotsk

coast the Even's main occupation is fishing and sea-hunting. Inland Even hunt squirrels, reindeer, elk, mountain sheep and bears. Until recently, furs brought in 90 per cent of their income. Traditionally there has been trade between the coastal and the inland Even. The fishers supplied the hunters with sealskin which was used for deer lassos, soles for shoes and other items. In return the nomads would provide venison and deerskin. Birchbark tents were the common form of dwelling. The Even believe in 'master' spirits of the mountains, hills, water and other natural phenomena. They also practise an ancient bear-cult and worship the sun. At Even festivals a huge round-dance is often performed.

GILYAK see NIVKHI

GOLDE see NANAI

GOLDI see NANAI

ITEL'MEN *Population:* 1,300. Language group: Paleo asiatic. The Itel'men are the ancient population of the Kamchatka peninsula in the extreme north-east of the USSR and were formerly known as Kamchadel. The term 'Itel'men' means 'resident' or 'living man'. They frequently inhabit river areas where they fish for salmon with nets and hooks. Hunting for fur-bearing animals is another important occupation. No other northern Siberian people engage so much in gathering wild plants. Grass, berries, and roots are an important part of their diet. Nowadays most Itel'men live on fishing collectives and use modern fishing methods. The Itel'men are shamanists and believe in evil mountain and forest spirits.

ITKANTSI see KORYAK

JEWS *Population:* 980,000. Languages: Russian and Yiddish. The Jews have a history of persecution by the Tsars which caused many of them over the centuries to go to

Siberia as refugees. Before the Revolution of 1917 they followed the only professions allowed them which were commerce and small trading. When the Soviets came to power, they wanted to establish a Jewish Autonomous Region, along the lines of the autonomous regions given to other nationalities. They decided on Birobighan, and tried to attract other Jews, especially from the Ukraine, to move there. However out of a total of nearly 3 million, only a few tens of thousands ever went to Birobighan, and many of these left after Stalin's death. Today only about 15,000 Jews remain there out of a population of about 150,000 in the Jewish Autonomous Oblast, the others living in other parts of Siberia. In contrast to the Soviet nationalities' policy, which encourages local newspapers and the teaching of traditional languages, there are no schools in Birobighan where either Yiddish or Hebrew are taught.

KAMCHADEL see ITEL'MEN

KAMENTSI see KORYAK

KARAGASI see TOFALAR

KARAGINTSI see KORYAK

KERET see KORYAK

KET *Population:* 1,200. Language group: Paleo asiatic. The Ket live in the Turukhanskii and Yartseuskii Regions along the Yenitsei river in southern Siberia. The word 'ket' means simply 'person' or 'man'. The Ket language is distinctly different from all neighboring languages. They hunt foxes, ermine, squirrels and wild reindeer for their furs, skins and meat. Nowadays they trap and hunt on the collective farms, where they also grow potatoes, carrots and cabbages. They

trade furs for flour. Ket are expert fishermen and use canoes made from hollowed-out tree trunks. They are shamanists, and also worship the bear.
(pages 124-125)

KHAKASI *Population:* 65,000. Language group: Turkic. The Khakasi live in the Khakasi Autonomous Oblast in the Minusa basin in southern Siberia. This is a semi-desert area of mountains and grasslands. The name covers five Turkic-speaking groups: Kachin (Khaas), Sagai, Bel'tir, Kyzil and Koibal. Settlement started there as early as 2,000 BC. The Khakasi were once nomadic pastoralists but are now based on collective farms where they herd sheep, goats, cattle and horses. The Kyzil have always been relatively settled in permanent villages. They were hunters and fishermen and also cultivated many field crops. Many Khakasi now work in gold and coal mines, and have been fairly well integrated into industry. They are shamanists who make images of spirits and 'feed' them in order to be free of misfortune and to ensure a good harvest.

KHANTI *Population:* 21,000. Language group: Finno-Ugric. The Khanti live to the east of the Ural mountains along the River Ob' and its tributaries in western Siberia. This is the Khanti Mansiski National Okrug. These traditionally nomadic horse-breeders, hunters and fishermen now operate from collective farms and are generally more settled. For travel on the river Khanti use canoes made from hollowed-out tree trunks. The northern Khanti use reindeer sleds all year round. In summer they live in tents but move in winter to huts made from thick boards. The Khanti are divided into clans. They are shamanists and each clan has its own ancestor cult. They have clung to their religion in spite of efforts to convert them to Christianity. The Khanti also have a vast mythology of legends and tales of their glorious warrior past.
(pages 48-51)

KORYAK *Population:* 7,400. Language group: Paleo asiatic. The Koryak live in the Koryak National Okrug on the Kamchatka peninsula in the extreme north-east of the USSR. In the past Koryak were divided into nine territorial groups. They were Charchuven, who were reindeer breeders; Kamentsi, who lived in Penzhina bay; Parentsi; Itkantsi; Apukintsi; Keret, a small coastal group who lived on the Bering Sea coast; Karagintsi; Palantsi; and the Alyutortsi, a large group that lived in the Kamchatka isthmus. The Koryak's main occupations are reindeer herding, hunting and fishing. The Palantsi in particular hunt foxes, wolverines, otters and ermine. The northern Koryak hunt seals and white whales. Reindeer provide the Koryak with meat, skins for clothing and housing, and tendons from which they make thread, besides being the main means of transport. They use grass to line their boots and to make mats, baskets and bags. The men carve bone and the horns of wild sheep. According to Koryak religion the world was once populated by a multitude of harmful spirits, *nin'vits*. Only the shaman can travel into the spiritual world and control them. Koryak also worship their ancestors and make wooden images of them. They also hold seasonal festivals and have various games and contests.
(pages 130-135)

KUMANDIN see ALTAI

139

MANEGRI see EVENKI

MANSI *Population:* 7,600. Language group: Finno-Ugric. The Mansi live in western Siberia along the River Ob' and its tributaries in the Khanti-Mansi National Okrug. Settlement in this area dates back to the Bronze and early Iron Ages. Horse breeding is their main occupation, but they are also expert trappers and hunters of reindeer, squirrels, otters, bears and other fur-bearing animals. Reindeer-skin tents are the summer dwellings of the Mansi, but they move to thin-beamed wooden huts in winter. Today they also grow vegetables on the collective farms. The Mansi are divided into clans and each clan has its own ancestor cult as well as an animal or bird totem. They are also shamanists and believe in another world of spirits.
(pages 48-51)

MONGOLS *Population:* over 3 million. Language group: Mongolian. The Mongols live scattered over immense territories of north, east and central Asia. Nearly a million live in the Mongolian People's Republic (formerly Outer Mongolia), but there are 1,800,000 Mongols in China, and about 315,000 Buriat (q.v.) Mongols in the USSR. Other groups live in Afghanistan, Tibet and India. The Mongols are descended from groups of nomadic herdsmen who lived on the steppes north and east of China. They lived in easily transportable tents, called *yurts,* and moved frequently from one pasture to another. At the beginning of the 13th century Genghis Khan rose to power and united them under the Mongol Empire. But a century later the Empire gradually began to fall apart. They were driven out of China in 1368, and succumed to the Manchu between 1691 and 1756, The fall of the Manchu dynasty in 1911 was seized by the Mongols as a chance of freedom. They had already been excited by the spirit of rebellion that spread through Russia in 1915, and now they drove out the hated Manchu and declared Mongolia autonomous, but it was still under powerful Chinese influence. In March 1921 a People's Government was appointed, and it called in the Red Army. In 1924 Mongolia was declared a Republic, along the Soviet model.

The traditional Mongol economy has always been based on herding and animal husbandry, and their staple food was mutton – preferably fatty mutton – in winter, and milk products in summer. Since World War II there has been industrial development and a rapid growth in a number of cities. Marriage has traditionally been monogamous, arranged by match-makers and including brideprice. Even today a Mongol will not marry someone closer than nine generations removed. Mongols are devoted to the 'three men's contests': horse-racing, wrestling and archery. In the past, lamaist Buddhism influenced much of the Mongol life, but since the revolution, the monasteries have gone the way of princes and serfs, and the people converted to socialism.
(pages 14-43)

NANAI *Population:* 9,900. Language group: Tunguso-Manchurian. The Nanai, who were formerly known as Goldi or Golde, inhabit the lower basin of the River Amur in southern Siberia. They also live on the island of Sakhalin, both along the coasts and inland. Nanai are first mentioned in ancient Chinese chronicles as far back as 2,000 BC and there are groups among them descended from the Chinese. Their main occupation is salmon fishing. In addition to food, these fish provide the Nanai with material for clothing and footwear. The Nanai now have modern fish canning plants and motor fishing stations for sea fishing. Inland Nanai are expert hunters and trappers. They hunt squirrels, sables, otters and foxes for their fur, and elk,

Siberian stags, deer and bears for meat. The blacksmiths among them make fishing-tackle, armor and helmets. They have also acquired great skill in boat-building and sled-making. Nanai dress includes ornate robes and silks, many of Chinese origin. They decorate most of the objects in daily use with ornamental carvings. They are shamanists and believe in 'master' spirits. Many possess ikons with pictures of shaman spirits.

NEGIDAL *Population:* small. Language group: Tunguso-Manchurian. The Negidal live on the Rivers Angun and Amur in the Kharbasouskil Kray in the eastern USSR. They hunt and fish for salmon and sturgeon. Their traditional way of life is now carried on in the collective farms. The summer tents give way to winter dwellings of bark, with a pointed, sloping roof. The women gather different kinds of berries to supplement the fish and venison diet. During the last century most Negidal clothes were made of fish skin. The Negidal are divided into clans, each with its own ancestor, ancestor spirits and communal clan prayers which are said before the hunting season. All Negidal celebrate the bear festival. Two important villages were flooded out in 1943 and all Negidal inhabitants went to join up with Russians in joint collective farms. They now farm and breed animals more than in the past and have been heavily influenced by Russians. The Negidal are now so few in number that they were not listed in the 1970 census.

NENTSI *Population:* 29,000. Language group: Samoyedic. The Nentsi are the largest of the Samoyedic speaking peoples. They have recently absorbed the Entsi, who once were their neighbors and reindeer herders like themselves. The Nentsi live in a large area of northern Siberia, but are particularly concentrated in the Nennish, the Taimyr and the Yamal Nennish National Okrugs, in the tundra and forest regions. The climate is harsh with long winters and strong winds and permafrost. Besides breeding and herding reindeer the Nentsi catch salmon and sturgeon in the local rivers and hunt squirrels, foxes, chipmunk, bears, ermine and elk for their furs and meat. Reindeer also provide meat, as well as lard and skins. The northern Nentsi were once nomadic, but have now settled in the collective farms, where they continue their traditional occupations, but also grow crops such as millet, wheat and

vegetables, Nentsi believe the mountains, rivers, lakes and trees have 'owner' spirits. The supreme god is called Num and his son, Nga, is considered an evil god who brings illness and death. The Nentsi employ shamans to consort and mediate with these spirits.
(pages 52-55)

NIVKHI *Population:* 4,400. Language group: Paleo asiatic. The Nivkhi were formerly called Gilyak. They live in eastern USSR, on the lower reaches of the River Amur and also on the island of Sakhalin. Nivkhi villages are usually situated near river mouths, and seldom exceed twenty dwellings. Fishing and hunting are their main occupations. They catch Siberian and humpback salmon with nets as well as with the more modern motor boats and winches. They also catch whales, walruses and sea-lions in quantity. The Nivkhi use dogs as draft animals and also for food and clothing. The number of dogs in a household is an indicator of wealth, and they are widely used as a medium for exchange. Nivkhi women process the skins of fish, seals and dogs. They also prepare birchbark, which has many uses, make the clothing and do housework. According to the Nivkhi every-thing has its spirit, even the island of Sakhalin itself. Every year the clan sacrifices a bear to its ancestors to pacify them and improve the fishing. They sculpt religious articles out of wood and bone.
(pages 126-129)

OROCHEN see EVENKI

OROCHI *Population:* 1,000. Language group: Tunguso-Manchurian. Most of the Orochi live in the villages near the mouth of the Turmin river in Kharbasovskii Kray in the far east of the USSR. They are hunters and fishermen who fish for salmon, sturgeon and carp. Nowadays most Orochi live on collective farms. There they keep cattle, pigs and horses, breed reindeer and employ modern fishing techniques. They also grow barley, wheat and millet. Many Orochi are skilled blacksmiths, and the women process fish skins and animal pelts and embroider clothes. Orochi are shamanists and believe everything has a spirit. They used to have special shrines where the shamans sacrificed pigs, roosters and dogs to their patron spirits. This was supposed to

ensure successful hunting and fishing. A variation of the same ceremony was performed to send off the souls of the dead to the other world. Only a few Orochi have been converted to Buddhism and Christianity.

OROK *Population:* 100. Language group: Tunguso-Manchurain. Virtually all the Orok live on the Val collective farm in the north-east of the island of Sakhalin off the Okhotsk sea coast. Their main occupation is reindeer breeding, and they also fish and hunt seal. Orok use the meat and the fat of the seal for food. In the past they also exchanged the meat for rice, flour, millet, cloth and tobacco. At Orok weddings reindeer were used as gifts to the bride's parents. It was the custom for the bridal train to travel by sleds which were harnessed to reindeer. The Orok believed their surroundings to be populated by spirits, to which sacrifices must be made. Orok also had cults associated with the bear and the killer whale.

PALANTSI see KORYAK

PARENTSI see KORYAK

RUSSIANS *Population:* 29 million in Siberia. Language group: Slavic. Russians have been coming to Siberia for centuries, for many different reasons and with varying degrees of official encouragement. The earliest migrants were religious dissenters who found refuge beyond the Ural mountains from religious persecution. They were extremely fanatical people who were willing to die rather than deny the beliefs and traditions of their sects. Among these *raskolniks* (dissenters) were the *dukhoborites,* Russian Quakers, *stundists,* who had special hours set aside for prayer and devotion, *molokists,* (milk drinkers) who were fanatical vegetarians, *khlusts,* who practised flagellation and other forms of self-mortification as part of their ritual, and *kamenshchiki,* who believed that the world was so evil that the only way to escape contamination was by complete isolation. By the end of the reign of Catherine the Great there were 30,000 such dissidents in Siberia. Other non-religious immigrants were those who were attracted by the furs of Siberia and the high prices they fetched in Moscow and St Petersburg. However, most of these were deterred by the natural hazards and obstacles which confronted travelers to the far north-east. In 1836 the Russian Tsar realized the immense strategic value of the vast territories beyond the Urals. He also sought to improve relations with China, particularly since Great Britain and other powers were developing far east connections. He appointed a governor for Siberia, and made his contribution towards its russification by sending a steady stream of prisoners and convicts, mainly political, but also criminal, into the Siberian wilds. By 1887 over 700,000 such prisoners had crossed the Ural mountains. It is not known how many survived, but the effect of the political prisoners, mostly of the intelligentsia and the upper classes, is clearly noticeable in Siberian society to this day. After the Revolution, the Soviet authorities were as fully aware as their predecessors of the strategic importance of Siberia, and carried on the plans to increase its Russian population. Political prisoners continued to be sent to camps, but their forced labor was put to use on five-year-plan projects. Other new arrivals were demobilized soldiers, who were rehoused in semi-military camps, especially along the Amur river, as a kind of potential militia in case of troubles. Voluntary immigrants of recent years have included large numbers of young Komsomol members, motivated by ideological indoctrination and a pioneering spirit. There were also those who were attracted by the government's concessions to new arrivals in Siberia, such as tax relief for small farmers and free housing. Today Russians are the majority of the population in Siberia, particularly in the towns. Great Russians have tended to settle in the Amur region and western Siberia, the White Russians further east, and the Ukrainians have settled mainly in the Ussuri river valley. Today, because of the constant migration and the relatively high birth rate among them, and the slow decline in numbers of the native tribes 97 per cent of the Siberian population are Russians. In the last 15 years several hundred new towns and settlements have been built, and more Russians are pouring in, prepared to brave the harsh climate for considerable material benefits.
(pages 78-103)

SEL'KUP *Population:* 4,000. Language group: Samoyedic. The Sel'kup, formerly known as Ostyak, live mainly in Tomskaya

Oblast and the Yamal Nennish National Okrug in northern Siberia. Their age-old occupations are hunting and fishing. Northern Sel'kup also breed reindeer and use them for transport. They use many hunting and trapping techniques to catch bear, elk, fox, squirrel and many other animals. Archaeology indicates that their ancestors appear to have lived underground in man-made caves. They believe in 'master' spirits and make sacrifices to them.

SHOR *Population:* 16,000. Language group: Turkic. The Shor live on the Kuznets Alatau and on the middle reaches of the River Tom in southern Siberia. This is a mountainous region, but is also the center of a famous industrial region, the Kuzbass. In the 17th century the Shor were blacksmiths, but they have since turned to farming on the gentler mountain slopes, and grow wheat, barley and hemp. They also hunt and fish. The Shor are shamanists and make offerings to the 'master' spirits of the mountains and forests to ensure their successful hunting, The Shor had an ancient custom of burying bodies in trees, wrapped in birchbark. This custom ceased in the 19th century.

TATARS *Population:* 120,000. Language group: Turkic. The west Siberian Tatars live mostly in rural localities in the Novosibirsk and Omsk area. They call themselves Tobolik, Tarlyk and Baruba Tatars. They are mainly farmers who grow wheat, barley, rye and oats. Some fish in lakes, while others raise horses. They once traded with central Asia by caravan. Tatars are Sunni Muslims, but also retain some shamanistic beliefs, especially in the 'master' spirits.

TELENGIT see ALTAI

TELESI see ALTAI

TELEUT see ALTAI

TOFALAR *Population:* 1,000. Language group: Turkic. The Tofalar call themselves Tubular and are also known as Karagasi. They live on the northern slopes of the

eastern Sayan mountains and on the upper reaches of the Rivers Uda, Iya and other left bank tributaries of the Ob'. Formerly nomadic herders, they now have farm cooperatives for hunting and reindeer breeding. They hunt bears, stags, elks, sables and squirrels. Tofalar women gather forest produce, especially berries, garlic, rhubarb, wild onion and cedar nuts. The Tofalar are shamanists who believe that spirits have to be kept satisfied to ensure successful hunting. The Tofalar shamans have special robes and tambourines.

TSAATANG *Population:* 300. Language group: Turkic. The Tsaatang live in the far north-western corner of the Mongolian People's Republic. They have not become Mongolized and retain their hard, nomadic way of life. Alone among the peoples of Mongolia the Tsaatang are reindeer-herders, and that is the meaning of their name. This had led to speculation that their original home was much further north, in Siberia. The economic unit was traditionally the family, which inherited the right to use certain clan pastures in the male line. Wives were taken from a different clan. The dwelling was a tent of long poles covered with birch-bark. Nowadays it has been replaced by cloths, skins and canvas sheets. The reindeer are hardly ever slaughtered for meat, and reindeer milk and its products are the staple foods. In winter the men go hunting and the

women look after the herds. The Tsaatang are not Mohammedan like most Turkic peoples, but shamanist, like most Siberian peoples. The Buddhist lamas reached the region, but had little influence there.
(pages 74-77)

TUBULA see ALTAI

TUBULAR see TOFALAR

TUNGUS see EVENKI

TUNKA SOYOT see BURIAT

TUVINTSI *Population:* 139,000. Language group: Turkic. The Tuvintsi are the major group living in the Tuva Autonomous Oblast in southern Siberia. They are mostly pastoralists who raise goats, sheep, cattle horses, camels, reindeer, yak and pigs on the collective farms. New crops, especially potatoes, have been recently introduced as well as modern machinery. The Tuvintsi also hunt and fish. Their homes used to be made of wooden frames covered with felt or reindeer skins. They are expert blacksmiths and woodcarvers. Although nominally converted to Buddhism, Tuvintsi retain their shamanist beliefs and practices.
(pages 106-109)

UDE see UDEGE

UDEGE *Population:* 1,400. Language group: Tunguso-Manchurian. The Udege live in the Khabarovskii Kray and Maritime Kray, near Vladivostok in the far east of the USSR. Udege life is based on hunting and fishing. They hunt deer, elk and bears for meat, and sables and raccoons mainly for fur. They do not hunt tigers as these are considered sacred. Udege women make things from animal and fish skins, and are expert embroiderers. The men are blacksmiths who manufacture household articles and hunting gear. Udege are known as the 'small people' of the Soviet

143

east: the men average a height of 5′ 3″, the women only 4′ 9″. Communal affairs used to be managed by a council of elders, and spoils from the hunt were shared equally among the villagers even before the Revolution. Udege are talented story-tellers, and in their spare time sculpt in wood and bone. They are shamanists and their most honored 'master' spirit is 'bua', the spirit of the taiga and the universe.
(pages 104-105)

UL'CHI *Population:* 2,400. Language group: Tunguso-Manchurian. The Ul'chi live in the Ul'chskii Raion of the Khabarovskii Kray in the eastern USSR. All their settlements are along the River Amur. They call themselves the Nani. The Ul'chi mainly fish for salmon, sturgeon and carp in the Amur, and they use nets, spears and hooks. Hunting for meat and fur is of secondary importance. Nowadays the Ul'chi diet is supplemented by agricultural produce and dairy products from their cattle herds. Fish is eaten raw, boiled or fried. It is also frozen, cured and smoked. The women process fish skins for clothing and footwear. They also weave mats and baskets from rose willow root. The men carve intricately with birchbark for boxes, instruments and boats. According to the ancient beliefs of the Ul'chi, stones, woods and water have spirits. Sacrificès were made to these spirits so that they would send game and fish.

YAKUT *Population:* 295,000. Language group: Turkic. The Yakut are the main native population of the Yakut ASSR, which is territorially one of the largest republics in the Soviet Union. They occupy the basin of the Middle Lena in eastern Siberia. For centuries they were mainly pastoralists and were thus distinguished from their neighbors. Now they herd cattle, horses and reindeer in the north. Before they moved into collective farms, they had summer and winter camps and moved seasonally. Yakut are expert fishermen, catching carp and white salmon in the rivers and lakes. They also hunt for meat and fur. The women gather pine sapwood for storage. Many Yakut are expert woodworkers and make their own utensils, crockery and furnishings. Others are blacksmiths making implements and weapons. They also carve from the ivory tusks of mammoths. Some Yakut today work in factories and mine the rich mineral deposits of the area. They have mongoloid features and practise shamanism.
(pages 56-69)

YUKAGIR *Population:* 600. Language group: Paleo asiatic. The Yukagir live in the far east of the USSR, along the tributaries of the River Kolyma-Korkodon, and in the foothills of the Aga Ts'a in the Yakut ASSR. They are hunters and fishermen. They mainly hunt wild reindeer. In winter Yukagir used to live in log huts, and in summer moved to tents covered with reindeer skins. They now live on reindeer-breeding collective farms. They are shamanists. At one time dead shamans were worshipped and offered sacrifices. Their bodies were dismembered and the parts kept as relics. Of all animal cults, that of the elk was most important.

(All population figures are approximate)

144